DISCARD

Fictional Structure and Ethics

Fictional Structure & Ethics

THE TURN-OF-THE-CENTURY

ENGLISH NOVEL

. .

.

William J. Scheick

THE UNIVERSITY OF GEORGIA PRESS   ∴   ATHENS & LONDON

© 1990 by the University of Georgia Press
Athens, Georgia 30602
All rights reserved
Designed by Louise M. Jones
Set in 10/14 Trump Mediaeval
The paper in this book meets the guidelines for permanence and durability of
the Committee on Production Guidelines for Book Longevity of the Council
on Library Resources.

Printed in the United States of America
94 93 92 91 90   5 4 3 2 1

Library of Congress Cataloging in Publication Data
Scheick, William J.
Fictional structure and ethics : the turn-of-the-century English novel /
William J. Scheick.
p.   cm.
Includes bibliographical references.
ISBN 0-8203-1242-8 (alk. paper)
  1. English fiction—20th century—History and criticism.   2. English fiction—
19th century—History and criticism.   3. Ethics in literature.   4. Literary
form.   I. Title.
PR888.E7S34   1990   823'.809353—dc20
90-30055   CIP

British Library Cataloging in Publication Data available

For Catherine

and for Jessica and Nathan

Contents

Introduction

At present, the English novel at the turn of the nineteenth century is, as a class, much undervalued by literary
critics. This book is designed to reevaluate the fiction of this
period, to define more precisely its place in the history of the
novel, and to offer new readings of some classic and some neglected works. This study includes an essentially three-tiered
argument: (1) that in the novel, as a literary form, structure
and characterization often vie for dominance; (2) that in many
novels evincing either a straightforward or a latent concern with
ethics, structure tends to be privileged; (3) that the momentous
change evident in the English novel from the turn of the nineteenth century to the modern period can be reinterpreted in
the light of the tension between fictional structure and characterization as well as in the light of the correlation between
fictional structure and ethics.

In brief, I argue that during the turn of the nineteenth century there were a number of English novelists, frequently clas-
sified as Post-Victorians and Edwardians, who experimented
more with fictional structure than with characterization, the
principal interest of the succeeding generation of writers, frequently called Modernists. Moreover, these turn-of-the-century
novelists often specifically focussed on the relationship between fictional structure and ethical concerns. I shall refer to
these authors as turn-of-the-century writers rather than as Post-
Victorians or Edwardians, and I try to avoid the word *Modernists* as much as I can or at least to qualify it when I am rarely

compelled to use it. These conventional terms are very problematic by now because they are encumbered by so many associations and vexed by our current understanding of the polysemous nature of fiction in all phases of its history. The writers at the center of my study are the ones Virginia Woolf felt that she and those sharing her literary interests were displacing in their own work. These turn-of-the-century authors did not actually form a selfconscious school of literary practice, but they were dominant in their day, often dialogued together, reinforced each other, and informally shared a number of artistic interests and techniques.

In stressing these turn-of-the-century English authors my discussion runs the risk of seeming to imply that the art of the novel as practiced by them is intrinsically superior to that of earlier and later writers, especially those of the modern period. I am particularly sensitive to the possibility that my description of Virginia Woolf's views of the novel and of the restrictions her mode of characterization places upon the reader might be construed as an attack on her art. And, worst of all, my emphasis on a correlation of fictional structure and ethics in turn-of-the-century novels possibly suggests the authority of the text, in contrast to the devaluation of such textual dominion in fiction by Woolf and others who share her ideas about literary art;[1] this implication of authority might be construed as a covert defense of the patriarchal hegemony evident in the novels at the center of my study. None of these three implications corresponds with my intention.

I single out Woolf in my opening chapter because she is a wonderful example of the novelist in reaction to these turn-of-the-century novelists and because in "Mr. Bennett and Mrs. Brown" she has given us a particularly articulate statement of emancipation that is useful in reconsidering her predecessors. In picking at her views in that statement I might seem somehow to denigrate her own achievements, but in fact I am not judging her art or her feminist politics. I only try to recover a phase in the history of the novel, the heritage of certain turn-of-the-century English novelists that has become somewhat obscured because the views of later authors, like Woolf, have prevailed (rightly or wrongly or indifferently). Although the force of my argument will doubtless take on a tone of advocacy, my objective is not to champion these novelists' specific practices or views. Rather I urge the recognition of the legitimacy of their artistic practice within the tradition of the novel and encourage a better appreciation of the heritage of their example in the novel as written today.

I am not neutral, of course. No act of criticism is without personal implications, even ethical ones, for the critic. As Wayne Booth has recently and forcefully reminded us, making ethical judgments in response to a text is not only a most natural act for the human mind, it is also an inevitable one; for readers make spiritual and emotional use of what they encounter.[2] I admit that underlying my discussion is a personal appreciation of what the turn-of-the-century novelist achieved. But this appreciation, and my desire to share it in making a case for the recognition of the place of the turn-of-the-century English novelist in the dynamic tradition of the novel, are not intended to imply the superiority of their work, in comparison to that of others, including Woolf. We know better than ever before, thanks to feminist scholarship, that Woolf's remarkable writings also represent a very important moment in the history of the novel.

The turn-of-the-century authors identified as Edwardians by Woolf—and Henry James is certainly *not* among them—usually receive less attention today as serious practitioners of the art of the novel partly because they *seem* to us, in the 1990s, less our contemporaries both in the methods and the purposes of their fiction. I suggest, however, that these writers held a legitimate view of the nature of fiction, practiced the *art* of fiction, furthered a tradition of fiction into our very own time, and can still speak to us whenever the techniques and ethical designs of their fiction potentially urge us to reflect.

My claims in this book about reflection in the reader, apropos of the correlation between fictional structure and ethical message, are influenced by reader-response criticism. This critical approach underlies principally two notions in my study: that fictional structure shares with architecture the primacy of the observer (reader), for whom it is ideally simultaneously aesthetic and instructive; and that the ontological and epistemological crisis of the turn-of-the-century period apparently encouraged some of its writers to think of their audience, with "a hungry credulity about new things" (in G. K. Chesterton's apt phrase), as more open to thought than it might have seemed in earlier times, when received cultural orthodoxy might have more readily shut their ears.

Although the presence of the early Stanley E. Fish might be somewhat in evidence in my readings, my approach belongs to no particular school of reader-response criticism. However, it conforms generally to the principles established by Wolfgang Iser, who has argued that "texts" involve readers in the production of meaning in such a way that readers in effect complete a literary "work." The process whereby a text evokes a response from the reader, Iser explains, is "virtually hermeneutic." This process causes the reader to "draw . . . new boundaries": "Every text we read draws a different boundary within our personality, so that the virtual background (the real 'me') will take on a different form."[3] Reference here is made to implied ideal readers, not necessarily actual readers. The exemplary reader of my own book will keep in mind that when I speak of the reader of turn-of-the-century fiction I always mean the *implied reader*, the

Introduction

ideal reader suggested by the semiotic codes of the text, particularly the codes I try to decipher in the structure of these works.

The term *structure*, I sometimes think, has become for critics principally an enabling reference. This pattern suggests that the meaning of this word tends to vary in accord with the critical system that appropriates it. I believe, however, that whatever system employs the term, informing that appropriation is a generally shared sense of the concept of structure, a sense defined by such structuralist theoreticians as Ferdinand de Saussure: that structure is not an insignificant mechanical ordering device, but something bearing meaning and value because it emerges from a system of options and is defined against a background of other possibilities. It has, in short, a vital human context (options), in terms of which it signifies meaning of some kind.

Although I principally rely on this general Saussurean sense of structure, I do venture a distinction between two features of literary organization: plot-structure and narrative-structure. Plot-structure is the shape of the *eventuation* of action in a story, whereas narrative-structure is the shape of the *telling* of the story—a distinction particularly explored in Chapters 2, 3, and 4. Perhaps this distinction can be read as my modification of the Russian Formalist contrast between *fabula* (fable; what happened) and *sjuzet* (discourse; narrative manner). Although in my study I emphasize the pattern of narrative-structure as a particularly cogent embodiment of authorial ethos, the design of plot can sometimes be a significant consideration, as Peter Brooks especially has observed,[4] when it serves as an index to deep-seated human tensions, compulsions, resistances, and desires.

Beyond my formulation of the difference between narrative-structure and plot-structure I am reluctant to go. Since the structure of a work can be a fairly stable architectonic, as some

Neo-Aristotelians prefer, or a shadowy chimera, as some decon-
structionists prefer; since literary structure can be consciously
designed, as some New Critics claim, or unconsciously repre-
sentational, as some New Historicists assert, I aim in my study
for a very flexible sense of how fictional structure actually manifests itself within the broad Saussurean definition of the term. I
hope that the nature of structure, as a polymorphous component
of the novel, will in the process of incremental demonstration
become empirically reified as my chapters progressively explore
the relation between fictional structure and ethics.

When thinking about the definition of the word *ethics* I sym-
pathize with the Supreme Court Justice who said, on a related
matter, that he could not quite say what it was, but that he
knew it when he saw it. Here that will not do, of course. Un-
fortunately, however, some of the best thinkers on the subject
of ethics have thrown up their hands in despair over the effort
to narrow the definition of this concept. J. Hillis Miller, for
instance, understandably concludes that the subject of ethics
finally "is one that cannot be adequately discussed in the ab-
stract. It *must* be analyzed and demonstrated in terms of specific
cases."[5] Given this affliction of generality when defining ethics,
perhaps one of the best statements about ethics that would also
apply to my sense of it in this book can be found in Dioge-
nes Laertius's quotation from Epicurus: "Ethics deals with the
things to be sought and things to be avoided, with the ways of
life and with the *telos* [the aim of life]."[6] Ethics, in this classical
sense, pertains to human options as well as to how those options, as expressions of valuation, open up or close down other
options. The emphasis in my book on ethics as the province
of human options coalesces with the emphasis in my book on
structure as something which emerges from and is defined by
these human options.

Introduction

In this study the testing-ground for my theories about the art of fiction as practiced by the turn-of-the-century novelist is primarily restricted to the ethical concepts of Christian-humanist and Schopenhauerian compassion. At the core of these two beliefs, involving profound human options, lies a shared sense that some things should be sought and some things should be avoided in the conduct of human life. What constitutes those options, as we shall see, differs depending on the operative notion of compassion. Nevertheless, the issues involved in the ethical exercise of options within these two fields of reference remain complex, especially as embodied in fiction. My hope therefore resides, as J. Hillis Miller suggests it must, in the expectation that the concepts of ethics and structure in my study will assume an emergent empirical presence in the process of my incremental demonstration and analysis of their mutually constitutive presence in the specific novels under discussion.

In part, the range of structure and ethics remains so wide in my study because my critical approach to the works under review is not limited to a reader-response methodology. Throughout this book, in fact, a variety of literary-critical methods is evident. Besides implications appropriated from reader-response criticism, I find empowerment from historical contextualism (especially emphasizing Christian-humanist and Schopenhauerian notions at the turn of the century), formalism (something of Neo-Aristotelianism and New Criticism), and deconstruction (limitedly and particularly in the fourth chapter). I use whatever method assists me in the detection of the correlation of fictional structure and ethics in the novels under consideration. Such literary-critical eclecticism, even an integration of such apparent oppositions as formalism and deconstruction, has been defended, most recently in Jerome J. McGann's *Social Values and Poetic Acts*;[7] but I know that this method is disparaged in some circles. I found, however, that an eclectic approach to the problem at the center of this study proved very useful to me in fashioning my arguments.

Insofar as I am concerned with structure, I am discussing form; and insofar as I am concerned with ethics, I am discussing content. The New Critical concern with the relation between form and content emphasized the circular way in which content determined form or form determined content, producing the self-enclosed art work. My interest in content and form, however, emphasizes the way the reader can discover the meaning of the content through the form, the structure. If a "text," as Iser explains, has a potential "virtual dimension" (the "work," in Iser's terms), which is activated by the implied reader's interaction with the "text," then, I would argue, the structural components of this "text" play a central role in leading the implied reader to re-create and complete the "work." If in this ideal reader a virtual self comes into being, along with a new creative awareness of his or her options, then the principal vehicle, I believe, for this development is the structure of the art object. Structure provides certain codes enabling the ideal implied reader to discover/dis-cover the implications (ethical or otherwise) of the content.[8]

The codes of this structure can sometimes certainly be an unconscious representation and justification of the dominant component of the culture in which its author lives (as most New Historicists claim). But I would urge that we should grant the probability that a particularly creative or deep authorial mind is sometimes capable of consciously designing artistic structures that evince deliberate (intentional), if at times conflicted, reasoning about his or her time and art. After all, is not this very human capacity for reflexivity in, and for the structuring of, thought something we as critics, including the New

xvii
Introduction

Historicists, believe to be a characteristic of our own mental processes? Especially in turn-of-the-century narratives, I have found, such an authorially designed fictional structure (form) often seems to manifest codes (options) whereby an implied reader is urged to ponder the ethical matter (options) of the content of these works. Sometimes an intended structure mutates beyond an author's control because of conflicts in his or her thinking, resulting in unintentional structural codes. In both cases, however, these narratives are frequently charged with an intense conviction and urgency even when these works seem to conform to the most mundane, conventional, and apparently least intellectual genres of fiction.

As my previous books have taught me, every work of this sort incurs debts. I acknowledge my indebtedness to the University Research Institute of the University of Texas at Austin for a grant providing me with the valuable time needed to complete this project.

I am also grateful to my colleagues in the Department of English, University of Texas at Austin, for support of various kinds: James Duban, John Farrell, and Wayne Rebhorn. Support came as well from other colleagues and friends: Edward Davidson, University of Illinois at Urbana; Wendell V. Harris, Pennsylvania State University; and Bernard Rosenthal, State University of New York at Binghamton.

Since publication is a strong incentive, I wish to thank editors O. M. Brack, Jr., Gerald A. Kirk, William Kupersmith, Robert Langenfeld, and Steen Holst Spove for publishing earlier versions of portions of this study. I am most indebted to the late H. E. Gerber, whose strong encouragement of my work on turn-of-the-century figures accounts for this book as much as does any other factor; and to Robert Langenfeld, whose work with

English Literature in Transition has not only carried on Gerber's heritage but even improved upon it.

I am especially grateful to Catherine Rainwater, who aided and abetted me in so many important ways.

Fictional Structure and Ethics

CHAPTER ONE

.   .

.

Fictional Structure
and Ethics

Our time, at the close of the twentieth century, is as peculiarly liminal as was the close of the nineteenth century. There is today, among some, an anxiety over what is seen as absorbing self-interest, a crisis in ethics, and a paralyzing individual uncertainty and indifference very similar to the concerns of many turn-of-the-century English authors. Several of these authors turned to fiction as a way of depicting, lamenting, decrying, or modifying the seeming direction or non-direction of their time. So we today are now well situated for a thoughtful reevaluation of the turn-of-the-century heritage of English fiction, especially its experimentation with structure to communicate ethical points-of-view to a transitional age which seemed to many of the novelists of that time to be on the edge of either a new potentiality or (more likely) a dire bankruptcy.

A large number of historians and literary scholars have described this time of transition, and collectively their findings indicate that it was indeed a period of conflict, ambiguity, and ambivalence. One can focus on the redirection of English attention away from the fading empire and toward discord and muddle at home, or on the secularization of religion, the rise of the cult of personal relations, and the discovery of the subconscious, among many other new developments,[1] but finally we never quite attain a full sense of how the perceived changes and complexities of the turn of the century generated what John Batchelor aptly calls an epistemological crisis in English culture at that time. It was a time, Batchelor concludes, when moral horizons contracted, former certainties eroded, and humanity was left with only the uncertain self as the new authority.[2]

In his autobiography Gilbert K. Chesterton gives a good impression of that time, and it might be useful to recall briefly some of his observations to establish a context for the focus of this study on the turn-of-the-century English novelists' concern with ethics. Although Chesterton typically warns his reader that he speaks finally about himself, he clearly indicates that his perceptions as a young man were culturally prevalent.

"Mine was the time of Impressionism," Chesterton recalls, "and nobody dared to dream there could be such a thing as Post-Impressionism or Post-Post-Impressionism." The significance of Impressionism for Chesterton lay in its characteristic representation of the 1890s and 1900s, "this age . . . of scepticism": "Its principle was that if all that could be seen of a cow was a white line and a purple shadow, we should only render the line and the shadow; in a sense we should only believe in the line and the shadow, rather than in the cow." This "highly subjective and sceptical . . . method of thought," Chesterton indicates, naturally lent "itself to the metaphysical suggestion that things only exist as we perceive them, or that things do not exist at all." In short, things which were once thought to be real were now perceived as mere "Illusion," and, Chesterton continues, "this atmosphere also tended to contribute, however indirectly, to a certain mood of unreality and sterile isolation that settled at this time upon me; and I think upon many others."

Fictional Structure and Ethics

A sense of the unreality of everything and a sense of the lonely isolated self (also unreal) in the face of this nothingness: little wonder, as Chesterton reports, that "the Decadents and the Pessimists . . . ruled the culture of the age," a time of "religious doubt, intellectual unrest, a hungry credulity about new things, and a complete lack of equilibrium."[3] And little wonder too that Chesterton identified this "contemporary nihilism," which seemed to him to be so prevalent during turn of the century, with the German philosopher Arthur Schopenhauer. References to Schopenhauer, whose work Chesterton almost certainly never read, occur time and again in Chesterton's books. In *Orthodoxy* (1908), for example, he refers to "the shrieks of Schopenhauer" driving humanity "to the emptiness of the asylum"; in *Manalive* (1912) he presents a professor who "sit[s] up all night" as "a student of Schopenhauer" and who must be frightened into discovering the "Will to Live"; and in *Come to Think of It* (1930) he refers to the turn-of-the-century period as "the time of the Schopenhauerian fashion."[4]

Schopenhauer's pessimism caught the mood of the time, at least among some intellectuals, and his thought infiltrated not only English culture during the turn of the century but also that of France and Germany, and, to a lesser degree, even America. The English translation of Schopenhauer's *World as Will and Idea* by R. B. Haldane and J. Kemp (1883–1886) went through many printings during the period. This translation, which appeared before the French version, was the primary means of the dissemination of Schopenhauer's influence on a number of turn-of-the-century authors.

As this study demonstrates, the ethical features of Schopenhauer's thought, particularly his notion of compassion, especially appealed to certain turn-of-the-century writers confronted with the sense of void described by Chesterton as characteristic of the times. So, to provide a grid for measuring the turn-of-the-century English novelists' management of fictional structure as a reflection of ethos, specifically the options facing humanity, I contrast two modes of compassion in the following chapters: the Christian-humanist and the Schopenhauerian. In many of the novels written during the turn of the nineteenth century one or the other of these concepts of compassion informs authorial point-of-view. The presence of Christian-humanist concepts in English fiction has in one way or another interested many literary critics, but Schopenhauer's development of these concepts has not received much attention, and the idea of Schopenhauerian compassion is virtually unknown.

As we shall see, an author's ethical concept of compassion can influence the techniques of any work of fiction he or she writes. Speaking of the matter of ethics and writing, and speaking of this concern in larger philosophical terms than I explicitly address in this book, J. Hillis Miller remarks, "Ethics and narration cannot be kept separate, though their [peculiar] relation is neither symmetrical nor harmonious."[5] This is an important observation, the first part of which expresses an idea appreciated by many novelists, particularly during the years 1880–1920. However, many of these same novelists, rightly or wrongly, did not anticipate Miller's second point about the lack of symmetry: that ethical closure for the reader is always frustrated by ambiguity. Moreover, even Oscar Wilde, a turn-of-the-century author who did hold such a view of problematical ethical closure, reminded his contemporaries that whatever a writer intends, readers extrapolate meanings, lessons, even morals from every text, regardless of an author's intent.[6] By accident, by association, or by design, narratives carry ethical implications.

At the turn of the nineteenth century, when so many of the traditional stabilities of culture seemed at risk or crumbling, a number of novelists consciously shaped their writings to reflect the anxiety-producing condition of the times, a reflection apparently often designed to cause *reflection* in the reader. A turn-of-the-century author might intend the reader's reflection, or self-conscious thought, to be merely a static apprehension (as in some of Wilde's fiction), or a sort of communal dirge for humanity (as in some of Joseph Conrad's fiction), or a call for reform (as in some of H. G. Wells's fiction). But in all instances, this reflection in the reader both "reflects" and "reflects on" human ideas, behavior, or options—that is, ethical concerns.

Ethical Veerings:
Stevenson and Wilde

Literary works certainly do not have to be ethical in intent to be serious art. They tend to be inherently ethical, however, because their province is human experience, their vehicle is human language with explicit or implicit idea-content, and their expression reveals the human relish for form—all three of which articulate with larger human cultural structures of the sort identified by the findings of, say, Claude Lévi-Strauss, Mary Douglas, and Victor Turner. When literature interacts with such larger anthropological or sociological structures it can polarize, at one extreme, toward community or, at the other extreme, toward the individual self. This privileging of community or of the self intrinsically involves ethical considerations, matters pertinent to the text being read and to the reader. This observation is supported by two turn-of-the-century romances, one by Robert Louis Stevenson and the other by Oscar Wilde.[7]

In *The Strange Case of Dr. Jekyll and Mr. Hyde* (1886), Jekyll's egotistic desire to transcend the flesh leads to "a life of extreme seclusion" in which "every act and thought centered on self." In contrast, Utterson, the narrator of the romance, maintains an equilibrium between his private desires and his need

"to see and touch his fellow-creatures." Utterson's balance between self and society emanates from his "approved tolerance
for others" and results in his benign function as "the last good
influence in the lives of down-going men."[8] Stevenson expertly
manages this thematic concern about balance by means of a
framing technique which culminates in the novel with the
reader reading what Utterson is reading of what Jekyll has written. By including the reader within this expanding community
of readers—that is, by the technique of an in-forming narrative-
structure expanding from within the text to include the reader
outside the text—Stevenson provides an ethical in-struction
conveying therapeutic instruction about each reader's experience of dual impulses in the self and each reader's need for active
membership in the human community.

Although it also depicts a Jekyll/Hyde duality in the self and
seems to accent the consequences of the egocentric pursuit of a
transcendent beauty beyond time and flesh, Oscar Wilde's Picture of Dorian Gray (1891) certainly differs from the sort of ethical concerns reflected in Stevenson's Strange Case of Dr. Jekyll
and Mr. Hyde. In the prefatory remarks he added to The Picture
of Dorian Gray after its appearance in Lippincott's Magazine in
1890, Wilde asserts that "all art is quite useless" and that "no
artist has ethical sympathies."[9]

Yet few readers close Wilde's book without a sense of some
moral. Whether Wilde's intention (at least as belatedly an-
nounced) successfully obviated in Picture what Wayne Booth
and J. Hillis Miller, in very different ways, ascertain as the intrinsic ethicality of all narratives is moot, whereas the fact that
most readers respond to the work as if it were ethical in message is empirically undeniable. Readers react in this manner,
Wilde explains in Intentions (1891), because in spite of what
an author intends or achieves, the reader reads ethical implications into a text. Objectively assessed, Wilde argues, art is like

experience, which is "of no ethical value"; art "has no influence upon action."[10] However this may be in objective fact, Wilde explains, people turn to art for patterns of behavior to imitate, and consequently they make their lives artlike.[11] Although the artist knows that generally readers behave in this way, he or she is obliged only to confront the "actual life . . . [of] chaos" by imposing a fabricated order upon it so that a nonethical apprehension of beauty might be better realized in the individual self and in society: "For the canons of good society are, or should be, the same as the canons of art. Form is absolutely essential to it."[12] Wilde's view expresses the post-Kantian understanding that humanity creates its own forms, which are not equivalent to some higher reality but which nonetheless aid in the disclosure of that reality. In this limited sense *The Picture of Dorian Gray* indeed exhibits an ethical structure implying an elusive moral or instruction. Within the text forms an in-struction providing a mirror in which the reader, in contrast to Dorian Gray's example, might sense some elusive reality within himself or herself, the source of all ethical concerns and patterns in society and in fiction. This in-forming structure urges the reader to experience his or her own, and hence humanity's, para-ethical desire for an ideal beauty.

The ethical dimension of literature, then, resides in the authorially crafted text and in the reader. Furthermore, as the examples of Stevenson's and Wilde's books indicate, this ethical dimension can be disclosed by the textual structure as perceived by the reader.

Many turn-of-the-century English novels tend to reflect this affinity between ethical considerations and fictional structure. Influencing this affinity is the tradition of allegory, which often evidences an inner structure reflective of ideal values.[13] More than a hint of the allegorical manner survives in turn-of-the-century novels. Even *The Picture of Dorian Gray*, so resistant to any certain single moral interpretation, possesses a structure derived from Wilde's self-conscious utilization of allegorical manner in the work.

Allegory does not dramatize human beings per se. It subordinates characters to a structural framework designed to make the reader examine the philosophical, social, theological, political, and even economic premises underlying human actions.[14] Turn-of-the-century English novelists, who inherited the tension between structure and characterization evident in Victorian fiction, generally veered toward structure and toward a typology of characterization. This accent on structure, rather than on in-depth characterization (to be discussed shortly), corresponds to their interest in the idea-content as well as in the generalized ethical context of their works. Such representative authors as Robert Louis Stevenson, Arnold Bennett, and H. G. Wells—however pessimistic they might be at heart—present an overview of their culture in the therapeutic hope of social melioration. This hope is always tentative or heavily qualified, to be sure, for these writers found themselves caught ambivalently between nostalgia for something irretrievably gone in their culture and acceptance of their para-cultural alienation from many of the same things.[15] That hope, no matter how it flickered or waned in their writings, nurtured their preoccupation with ethical concerns implicit in social structures and embodied in fictional structure. This stress on in-struction in society and texts, for the therapeutic purpose of instructing the reader, required the dominance of structure in their novels, a dominance at least favoring, if not requiring absolutely, a typology of characterization similar to the manner of allegory.[16]

A fin de siècle story can convey ethical implications even when it seems to be little more than an exercise in a conventional popular fictional genre. Consider, for example, an ostensibly very simple ghost-story by Rudyard Kipling.

Hesitation:
Kipling and James

Still too persistent in critical assessments of Kipling's work is the notion that his early stories are measurably less accomplished than his later tales. Elliot L. Gilbert, however, has demonstrated the error of this judgment, especially when his excellent study of Kipling's short fiction focuses on "Without Benefit of Clergy" (1890, 1891).[17] Arguing that this short story is not as simple as it appears on the surface—Gilbert is refuting J. M. S. Tompkins's assertion that the work requires no interpretation[18]—Gilbert emphasizes patterns of ritual behavior in the tale, patterns which comprise a complex network of mutually reinforced meanings pertaining to an indifferent universe in the story. Gilbert not only successfully demonstrates the richness underlying the "simple" artistry in one of Kipling's earliest tales, but he also implicitly instructs us to seek similarly adequate critical systems to unearth this sort of richness in other early fiction by Kipling. As Gilbert's attention to ritual in "Without Benefit of Clergy" suggests, finding a suitable critical stance, specifically an adequate critical vocabulary, makes a significant difference in assessing the artistic achievement of Kipling's fiction; and, as we shall see, this insight will in turn shed light on how a turn-of-the-century author can manage his narrative to reflect ethical concerns.

With Gilbert's example in mind, we may turn our attention to a very early story by Kipling that has been critically neglected: "The Phantom 'Rickshaw," which first appeared in *Quartette* (the Christmas annual of *Civil and Military Gazette*) in 1885 and was first collected in 1888. Regard for this story in Kipling's canon is curious. On the one hand, there are Kipling's own comments on the tale: in *Something of Myself* he says of the story that it was a "serious attempt," but "some of it was weak, much was bad and out of key"; in the Preface to an edition of *The Phantom 'Rickshaw and Other Tales* (1900) he says that the work "is not a very good specimen" of the ghost story, albeit "you can credit it from beginning to end."[19] On the other hand, there are the facts that Kipling himself still endorsed the story for inclusion in the last selection of his works that he authorized and that some editors of Kipling's stories have included "The Phantom 'Rickshaw" as an excellent representative of his short fiction.[20] Similarly, Kipling's contemporary critics, at one extreme, remarked that the tale should have been destroyed and, at the other extreme, thought the work was highly original.[21] Recent critics fairly routinely refer to it, usually in passing, as an interesting but minor work; they have not probed the story in any test of its artistry.[22]

To appreciate "The Phantom 'Rickshaw" we need a critical perspective as appropriate as is Gilbert's focus on ritual behavior in "Without Benefit of Clergy." For this purpose, we might turn as a place to begin to Tzvetan Todorov's idea of the fantastic. I stress *as a place to begin* because I do not wish merely to demonstrate how Kipling's story conforms to Todorov's theory. Rather, I want to use Todorov's structuralist concept as a point of entry in my exploration of the complexity of Kipling's art in "The Phantom 'Rickshaw" as an expression of an ethical viewpoint.

In order to qualify for the genre Todorov classifies as the fantastic, "The Phantom 'Rickshaw" must make the reader hesitate between a natural and a supernatural explanation of the events narrated, a hesitation which the reader usually shares with the protagonist of the story. Todorov explains, "The fantastic occupies the duration of this uncertainty. Once we choose one answer or the other, we leave the fantastic for a neighboring genre, the uncanny or the marvelous. The fantastic is that hesitation experienced by a person who knows only the

Fictional Structure and Ethics

laws of nature, confronting an apparently supernatural event."[23] Kipling's story of how Theobald Jack Pansay rejects his lover, who dies in grief and who *apparently* haunts him to his own death, satisfies Todorov's criterion for the fantastic. As readers of "The Phantom 'Rickshaw," we remain uncertain whether Pansay's experiences with the apparent ghost of Agnes Keith-Wessington are real encounters or hallucinations deriving from guilt over his callous treatment of her.

Arguing for one interpretation is Dr. Heatherlegh, who relentlessly insists that Pansay suffers from "too much conceited Brain, too little Stomach, and thoroughly unhealthy Eyes," that he suffers from "a Stomach-*cum*-Brain-*cum*-Eye illusion," which is medically treatable.[24] Pansay tries to accept this natural explanation, but everything he does in accordance with his doctor's instructions fails to result in a remission of these so-called "persistent 'delusions'" (p. 5). Through much of these encounters Pansay hesitates between a natural and a supernatural explanation of events: "Either that I was mad or drunk, or that Simla was haunted with devils" (p. 13). Just prior to his demise Pansay tends to believe that he is being punished as a "condemned criminal" (p. 5) for having caused Agnes's death (cf. p. 38).

"But you shall judge for yourselves" (p. 5), Pansay writes, and this important remark directs our attention to the readers of Pansay's narrative, which comprises most of the short story. Pansay's prospective readers include Kitty Mannering (p. 34), to whom he was engaged until she broke off the relationship and coldly rebuffed him (much in the same manner as he had rejected Agnes) when she learned about his treatment of his previous lover; his readers include the narrator, who "suggested that [Pansay] should write out the whole affair from beginning to end, knowing that ink might assist him to ease his mind" (p. 4); and his readers include us. We identify with the narrator, whose framing introductory remarks Kipling cogently added in a revision of the story;[25] with the narrator we hesitate as we struggle to judge for ourselves whether Pansay's experiences are real or imaginary. Like the narrator we remain uncertain. Like the narrator we are unable to accept Dr. Heatherlegh's natural explanation (which would make the tale uncanny—that is, according to Todorov, its strangeness explained by physical or mental causes) because Pansay enjoys "perfect health" and "a well-balanced mind" (p. 11), because none of the doctor's cures succeed, and because even full confession fails to remedy the problem. Like the narrator, we are also unable to accept Pansay's final supernatural explanation (which would make the tale marvelous—that is, according to Todorov, its strangeness explained by spiritual causes) because neither we nor anyone other than Pansay in the story have seen the ghosts. As Todorov observes, "Either total faith or total incredulity would lead us beyond the fantastic: it is hesitation which sustains its life."[26] As readers of "The Phantom 'Rickshaw" we are, like the narrator Kipling, eventually included in the narrative, someone with whose uncertainty we can identify; we continue to hesitate between a natural and a supernatural explanation of events.[27]

Todorov's structuralist paradigm takes us this far in appreciating Kipling's artful management of the revised version of "The Phantom 'Rickshaw." However, in stressing the reader's hesitation Kipling's narrative extends beyond Todorov's notion of the fantastic, for as readers we hesitate not only between a natural and a supernatural explanation of events, but also over the rightness or wrongness of Pansay's eventual sense of guilt in the story. This other mode of hesitation is important to remark because our inability to judge for ourselves and resolve this issue of guilt profoundly reinforces our uncertainty over whether the apparitions seen by Pansay are real or imaginary. The framing narrator clearly urges the reader toward a continued hesitation

over the matter of Pansay's guilt when he says in his introduc
tory comments that Pansay "may or he may not have behaved
like a blackguard to Mrs. Keith-Wessington" (p. 3). The narrator, deliberately added later to the story by Kipling, explicitly
indicates his reluctance or his inability to judge Pansay, whom
he knew well and whom he certainly knew better than we, the
readers, who ought to be at least as hesitatingly cautious as the
narrator in this matter of judging Pansay.

Consider Pansay's position. When he first met Agnes, he
and she fell "desperately and unreasonably in love with one
another" (pp. 5–6). He never planned to seduce and abandon
her; he had become infatuated—a human, natural occurrence.
After the love affair progressed for a while Pansay discovered
that he really did not love Agnes, that he had been only infatuated with her: "my fire of straw burnt itself out to a pitiful end
with the closing year" (p. 6). He has no early inkling of this outcome; but it happens, and he finds himself in an embarrassing
situation. He tells Agnes the truth and tries to end the affair.
Agnes, however, insists over and over that "it's all a mistake"
(p. 7) and asks Pansay to forgive her (what she asks forgiveness
for is never clear). Nothing will convince her that the affair is
over, and consequently Pansay's feelings evolve from "passive
endurance" to "blind hate" in combating her resistance to the
truth of the situation (p. 7). His rebuffs, never gentle even from
the first, become still more curt and cruel; although he realizes Agnes is the victim of his change of heart, he cannot help
but note that in the matter of his increasingly angry treatment
of her "she was much to blame" (p. 7). He later thinks that he
"might have been a little kinder to her," but he knows this idea
"really *is* a 'delusion'" (p. 7); for what was he to do in the face of
the reality of his dislike: "I could not have continued pretending
to love her when I didn't, could I?" (pp. 7–8).

The reasonable answer to Pansay's query is, of course, no, he could not continue with such a pretense. To have done so would have been a crime against himself and against Agnes. He did not "honestly, heartily" love her the way he comes to feel about Kitty Mannering (p. 8). So Pansay finds himself on the horns of a dilemma: either he must live a lie and be miserable (and perhaps make Agnes miserable too) or he must tell the truth and make her so miserable that she "haunts" him to a miserable end. Herein is the hub of the narrator's and our hesitation over Pansay's guilt, whether "he may or he may not have behaved like a blackguard to Mrs. Keith-Wessington."

This level of perception places the reader well beyond Todorov's structuralist paradigm of hesitation between a natural or a supernatural explanation of events; this initial uncertainty is now reinforced by our hesitation over the ethical issue of the rightness or wrongness of Pansay's guilt. From the vantage point of this deeper awareness of uncertainty we can penetrate Kipling's artistry still further in the tale if we realize that the very act of hesitation we are experiencing at two levels of the text informs the central meaning of the narrative. Although Pansay might or might not see ghosts and although he might or might not be guilty, he is at fault for having failed to pause —that is, he did not hesitate before beginning his desperate and unreasoned affair with Agnes, and he did not hesitate before hastily and curtly breaking off this affair.

His failure in the latter instance is mirrored in Kitty's curtness and lack of hesitation in breaking off her engagement to Pansay. He now finds himself feeling what Agnes must have felt; indeed, Pansay even repeats Agnes's refrain, "there is a mistake somewhere," and, as did Agnes with him, he begs Kitty to forgive him (pp. 26–27). The "mistake" to which he, Agnes, and Kitty obliquely refer, the mistake that requires forgiveness, is that Pansay had never hesitated to consider how Agnes would feel; as a result of an insensitivity that is certainly a flaw in his

character he could only at first feel a "pity . . . [of] passive endurance" toward her (p. 7). It is no accident that the final words
of his narrative emphasize compassion: "Pity me"; "in justice,
too, pity her" (p. 38). Had he felt real pity for Agnes earlier, Pansay would have paused before acting and, through reflection,
found a better way to handle the problem, other than relying
on curtness. The most he had been able to manage by way of
such reflection was a "feeling, *but only for a moment or two,*
that [he] had been an unutterably mean hound" (p. 9; emphasis
mine). Not until the "haunting" by Agnes or his dismissal by
Kitty has Pansay been a reflective man, or hesitated.

For, finally, in "The Phantom 'Rickshaw" to hesitate means
to reflect. The story suggests that before we act, before we judge,
we should hesitate—that is, enter into a liminal space where
time is arrested, where we can reflect before re-entering and
acting in the world. The pity Pansay asks for himself and Agnes
derives from this reflection to which he has been driven; and
compassion is what we and the narrator should feel for Pansay in spite of his initial insensitivity (a character flaw which
might or might not deserve such guilt that he dies from it). Like
the narrator, we hesitate, and in ethical reflection ideally find
compassion or pity in judging Pansay's guilt for ourselves. As
readers we should enact the very hesitation, with its ethical implication of compassion, that Pansay lacked at first and is driven
to at last, if too late.

In pausing before passing judgment on Pansay we hesitate to
pass judgment on ourselves; for the ethical point of Kipling's
story is that just as Pansay should have pitied Agnes, and Kitty
should have pitied Pansay, we and the narrator should pity
Agnes and Pansay. We are all in need of compassion in the wake
of life's events.[28]

This sense of the propriety of an essentially Christian-
humanist compassion lies at the heart of the function of hesita-

tion in "The Phantom 'Rickshaw." The ideal readers of the tale will pause over natural or supernatural explanations of events and over the rightness or wrongness of Pansay's guilt, finally to hesitate over their own hesitation; that is, these readers potentially become reflective as they (with the narrator) glimpse their own share in Pansay's and Agnes's human plight. These deepening layers of hesitation, conveying a turn-of-the-century ethical point about compassion, constitute the keen artistry of "The Phantom 'Rickshaw."

When we think of famous literary ghost stories published during the turn of the nineteenth century, Henry James's "Turn of the Screw" (1898) readily comes to mind, the stylistic and symbolic complexities of which certainly contrast with the seeming simplicities of Kipling's short story. There is a narrative layering in James's story which, like that of Kipling's, points to and implicates the reader, who is similarly forced to hesitate. Todorov was especially sensitive to James's work,[29] but his idea about the reader's hesitation over a natural or a supernatural explanation of what happens in such a story as "The Turn of the Screw" is again too limited. Although some critics would cite James in dismissing this story as a mere ghost story, or others would say that James's ethical message in the tale remains ambiguous from the first, possibly the reader of this tale might, as one critic has remarked, be instructed to hesitate over more than the mere issue of a natural or supernatural explanation of the events in the story, and specifically to ponder the relation of fantastic literature, superstition, and human violence.[30] Or, perhaps, the reader of this story is directed to ponder the very ethics of interpretation itself. Whether or not these are accurate responses, I think the reader of this Jamesian ghost story ultimately hesitates over the nature of literature itself, over the wondrous text of this narrative, whose very expression demands recognition as art from the reader. "The Turn of the

Screw" is indeed a marvelous example of literary artistry, and the reader finally hesitates, in awe, over the ingenuity of the narrative texture of this story. As a result, however, whatever ethical dimension James may have intended in "The Turn of the Screw" is displaced, or at least somewhat supplanted, by the reader's hesitation, or reflexivity, over the phenomenon of the text as aesthetic expression.

In contrast to the artistic opacity of James's short story, Kipling's "Phantom 'Rickshaw" is seemingly transparent and draws little overt attention to itself as narrative. Consequently, the ethical message of Kipling's ghost story is not displaced by the implied reader's final hesitation, in awe, over its self-reflexive manifestation of the *art of literature*, but is focused unobstructedly on that reader's eventual hesitation, in awe, over what humans do to each other or ideally can do, by way of options, in the *art of life*. James's short story might also exhibit the ethical nature of fiction, but Kipling's narrative more aptly illustrates the vital connection between life and art in the matter of ethical concerns. The urgency of such concerns appears even in seemingly simple turn-of-the-century narratives of a conventional type, in which (like Kipling's "Phantom 'Rickshaw") questions of ethics might at first be least expected.

James's tale is, many critics would agree, a greater work of art than is Kipling's. But if this is true, and if the contrast is not merely a matter of two very different kinds of artistry, a problem lies in James's greater achievement if we assess it from the point of view of authors sharing Kipling's sense of the ethical potentiality of fiction. In attaining for itself recognition from the reader as an epitome of superb literary art, it implies a preponderant importance for art as art, which position is at best ethically marginal. Such an ethically remote position finally tyrannizes over whatever other ethical implications may abide in James's story. For the attention of the reader is directed finally not to an experiential field of options in life but to the wondrousness of the story as literary contrivance.

So if "The Turn of the Screw" seems more accomplished as aesthetic expression than "The Phantom 'Rickshaw," Kipling's story seems more successful in artistically conveying an ethical purpose. Drawing virtually no attention to itself as narrative, Kipling's tale remains truer than does James's work to conveying an ethical design, assuming of course that the tale James said was merely a ghost story possesses an ethical message. The ethical function of fiction, as a reflection of and on the reader's options in life, was an urgently important matter to Kipling and to many of his fellow turn-of-the-century authors.

Fictional Structure and Ethics: James and Woolf

For many turn-of-the-century English novelists this emphasis on ethics is best embodied in the structure of fiction rather than in characterization. Characterization in some form occurs in all fiction, even in the *nouveau roman* where it certainly is minimal. Structure likewise occurs in all fiction, sometimes as a pronounced or as a latent architectural framework, at other times merely as plot, epiphanic moments, or a rhythm underlying a paratactic technique. Moreover, structure can determine characterization, or structure can be determined by characterization—and in this complex sense, the shaping of characterization can be said always to involve structure. However they may be bound together in the finished narrative, they also apparently exhibit an underlying tension.

When an author privileges (usually in-depth) characterization in fiction, the work tends to evince a weakening, delimiting, or even devaluation of architectural pattern as well as a tendency against characterization by type (caricature). This tendency is reversed when structure receives authorial stress. Then "the more the other narrative elements such as plot, commentary, description, allusion, and rhetoric must contribute to the work."[31] Structure and characterization appear to vie for dominance in fiction, and this dialectical behavior is perhaps appropriate for a genre so replete with antithetical elements that no poetics of the novel seems sufficiently inclusive.[32]

As J. Hillis Miller and others have shown, when in-depth presentations of complex characters rival structural patterns in Victorian fiction, the experiences of these characters expand narratively and press against the confines of fictional form.[33] For example, Lucy Snow's emotional intensity so engaged Charlotte Brontë that the plot-structure of *Villette* (1853) becomes distorted by improbabilities and incredible coincidences. William Makepeace Thackeray thought that Brontë had been too permissive with the protagonist of *Villette*,[34] and in contrast, in *Vanity Fair* (1847–48) he permitted the behavior of puppetlike Becky Sharpe, whose idiosyncrasies are never divulged, to be determined by the fated structural limitations of her stagelike world.

This tension between structure and characterization bedeviled not only Victorian novelists but their successors as well. In *Tono-Bungay* (1908), for example, H. G. Wells registers a fascination with his consistent first-person narrator, but structural considerations prevail, particularly a recurrent rise-and-fall pattern. This pattern holds in check all the characters in the novel until, as Wells himself later confessed, the book "present[s] characters as part of a *scene*."[35] In *Ulysses* (1922), on the other hand, James Joyce privileges interior characterization, which is reinforced by a loose dialogical structure providing no final word of resolution. This suppression of structure suits both Joyce's apparently detached comprehensive perspective and his preoccupation with open-ended human experience (character). Yet, as if certain of his aesthetic goals in *Ulysses* might be threatened by this open-endedness, he circumscribed his characters' activities with an appropriated Homeric framework. This mythic scaffold functions ironically, but finally its weightiness and artificiality in relation to the prevailing flow of the mundane experiences undergone by the characters in *Ulysses* suggest the difficulty of according equal emphasis to characterization and structure in a single work. And Virginia Woolf experienced similar problems, as her notebook with her plans for *Mrs. Dalloway* (1925) indicates. In this notebook she ponders the formlessness of her projected novel and wonders whether she could contain it within such formal, traditional structural devices as a recurrent observer serving as a Chorus-figure or a division of "the scenes . . . like acts of a play into five."[36]

From the 1880s to the 1920s some authors have explicitly remarked the tension between structure and characterization. Henry James, for instance, noted the problem in the Preface to the New York Edition of *The Portrait of a Lady* (1908). He admired this novel for its "structure reared with an 'architectural' competence"; yet, he remarked, "I would rather, I think, have too little structure than too much—when there's danger of its interfering with my measure of the truth." He had in mind the germinal stages of his novels, their origination in his seminal preoccupation with a "stray figure" or an "unattached character." James was, by his own admission, "much more antecedently conscious of his figures than of their setting"—what Wells referred to as the scene. James's "preferential interest" in characterization disturbed him as an example of "putting . . . the cart before the horse" and made him envy "the imaginative writer so constituted as to see his fable first and to make out its agent afterwards."[37]

James's sense of an antagonism between the restrictive architecture of the "fable" and the expansive truth of the stray, "unattached character" anticipates an observation made nearly fifty years later by William Faulkner. During an interview Faulkner indicated a conflict between his belief in the requirement that "each book had to have a design" and his recurrent experience of "point[s] in the book where the characters themselves rise up and take charge."[38] Like James, Faulkner experienced something of what M. M. Bakhtin categorized as heteroglossia, a multiplicity of character voices, essentially unresolvably dialogic and beyond an author's control.[39]

Brontë, Thackeray, Wells, Joyce, James, and Faulkner are diverse representatives of important novelists, from the Victorian through the modern periods, whose work evidences the tension between characterization and structure. In fact, the momentous time of transition in the novel, from 1880 to 1920, can be interpreted in terms of this tension. On the one hand, many of the turn-of-the-century novelists attempted to simplify the problem of their Victorian predecessors by emphasizing structure in their novels. Typically, Arnold Bennett maintained that the artist must possess "a deep love of form"; the novelist "can, by obtaining a broad notion of the whole, determine with some accuracy the position and relative importance of the particular series of phenomena to which his instinct draws him. If he does not thus envisage this immense background of his special interests, he will lose the most precious feeling for interplay and proportion."[40] Proportion, a feature of architectural design, is apparent in Bennett's *Anna of the Five Towns* (1902), which (as we shall see in Chapter 2) evinces the Freytagian pyramidal structure of classical tragedy, and in his *Old Wives' Tale* (1908), which exhibits a well-designed framework of parallel events. And as we earlier noted in passing, Wells's *Tono-Bungay*, which Bennett admired as a "distinguished and powerful book,"[41] structurally subordinates its characters to a "scene" defined by a recurrent rise-and-fall pattern.

On the other hand, the so-called Modernists attempted to simplify the problem of the Victorian novelists by emphasizing characterization in their fiction. They did so, as well, in conscious reaction to turn-of-the-century writers' stress on structure. In "Mr. Bennett and Mrs. Brown," first delivered as an address in 1924, Virginia Woolf surpasses James's desire not to hamper characters too much by structural design and focuses on characterization in the novel as an end in itself without saying a word about the overall shape or design of fiction. The Edwardians, most notably Bennett, Galsworthy, and Wells, according to Woolf, "laid an enormous stress upon the fabric of things. They have given us a house in the hope that we may be able to deduce the human beings who live there."[42] That she cares less for the house than for the people in it corresponds to her primary interest in characterization rather than in structure in her novels. This emphasis corresponds to a recent argument, expanding upon observations by Rachel Blau DuPlessis, that Woolf aimed at resisting tyrannical (patriarchal) narrative structural patterns by valorizing a subversive subjective lyricism expressive of repressed female desires.[43] Since no novel is completely devoid of structural particulars, it is not surprising to detect muted structural devices in Woolf's fiction. However, structure is only vestigial in her work, as even her notebook entries on *Mrs. Dalloway* reveal. For her, as "Mr. Bennett and Mrs. Brown" reports, "men and women write novels because they are lured on to create some character"; "it is to express character . . . that the form of the novel, so clumsy, verbose, and undramatic, so rich, elastic, and alive, has been evolved."

In contrast, she accuses, "the Edwardians were never interested in character in itself." But why is characterization in itself necessarily the greatest value in fiction, a view with which Henry James was sympathetic without taking such an extreme position? Woolf does not explain, nor does she even hint that the tradition of the novel only half supports her view. Wells, one of her targets who tended to subordinate characters to fictional structure, seems closer to the reality of the tradition of the novel when he suggests, even at the end of his long career, that the novel is essentially reactionary, protean, and inclusive: "a novel . . . could be any sort of honest treatment of the realities of human behaviour in narrative form."[44] Form gets the last word from Wells.

Nor does Woolf suggest that philosophical views and ethical concepts contribute to an author's decision to stress structure or character in a novel. This is an important point, central to the arguments of my book: that within the characterization-structure dialectic in the novel a positive correspondence frequently exists between authorial emphasis on fictional architecture and authorial interest in ethical concerns per se; these often didactic concerns evidence a profound interest in the preservation, melioration, or, simply, the depiction of human society.

This correspondence between structure and ethics is suggested in Walter Pater's *Imaginary Portraits* (1887), which indicates how during the nineteenth century architecture was perceived as a kind of communication designed to teach and to evoke response.[45] In architectural art, structure confronts and directs the viewer's eyes. This informing pattern, an inner structuralizing, or in-structing intimating some totality of effect, can be said to instruct the eye of the viewer.

Literary structure functions similarly. The conception of architecture as a means of communication applied as well during the nineteenth century to literary structure, the equivalent of architectural form. In novels structure contextualizes the other fictional elements and so orients the reader. Consider the following conclusion about an instance of literary structure: "As the spatial ekphrasis bounds the dynamics of the narrative formally, the use of space also elicits the ethical or moral, as well as the aesthetic significance of this text [*Daphnis and Chloe*]. As the spatial form causes the gradualness in the temporal narrative, so too does it mirror the ethical standard of the work, which may be summarized as the necessity of equating desire with need. One must bound temporal desire by restricted need as spatial form bounds temporal movement."[46] In a literary work as a whole, as well as in its specific content, variations in the management of structure emerge for similar didactic purposes. This tradition survived in the fiction of those turn-of-the-century English novelists preoccupied in some manner, however vaguely or dubiously, with social melioration. These writers were particularly sensitive to the correspondence between structure (designed to direct the reader's view) and ethics (the proposed object of the reader's attention). Just as architectural design can be beautiful and useful, fictional structure can be aesthetically in-forming and didactically instructive.

This equivalency derived from classical rhetorical tradition, and in the novel it came to include patterns of organization based on such specifically architectural features as repetition, parallelism, juxtaposition, enclosure, gradation, and antithesis as well as, in fact, on all variations (including distortions) of the principles of unity, scale, rhythm, proportion, and sequence.[47] Effect counts uppermost, for fictional structure shares with architecture the primacy of the implied observer, for whom it is (like its prototype) to be at once aesthetic and instructive. Wells had this relationship in mind when in a letter (8 July 1915) he told Henry James that "literature like architecture is a means, it has a use"; and when elsewhere he later expressed his preference for an "adjustment-interest in fiction" rather than for the "character-interest" so prevalent, in his opinion, not only in writings by James but generally in "the fiction of the nineteenth century and early twentieth century."[48]

Characterization and Ethics:
Brontë, Hardy, Joyce, Woolf

What about characterization; does it not also potentially instruct the reader? In responding to this query we might
observe that the Greek word *ethos* refers to trait, as in character trait, and then we might cite a passage from George Eliot's
defense of the art of fiction: "He who furnishes innocent amuse-
ment does something; he who draws a faithful picture of life
does more, but he who, whilst drawing the picture chooses
models who may elevate and improve . . . has reached the highest excellence in his art."[49] As George Eliot indicates, characterization can instruct, especially when readers pass judgment
on the human behavior dramatized in a novel. George Eliot's
comment about characterization, however, does not promise
that the reader will find it easy to assess behavior when it is
complexly portrayed or that everyone will agree upon what is
good. In fact, Victorian fiction is replete with difficulties of this
kind even when the overall ethical design of a work becomes
clear. When the ethical stance of an author remains inclusively
polymorphous, as in *Wuthering Heights* (1847), the problem of
character evaluation becomes even more difficult.

In Emily Brontë's novel characterization somewhat dominates. Violating structure, her characters represent an unresolved standard of ethics (options), save their representation of
individuality. Her narrative suggests that this ethical irresolution is a genuine communal value. A recent, cogent Bakhtinian
reading of this work concludes that Brontë's "novel maintains
its heteroglossia and refuses to be reduced to a unitary statement" and that consequently "instead of getting an explanation,
we get deeper into uncertainties of choice and interpretation":
"the contest of values in *Wuthering Heights* is not between
. . . two pairs of lovers. The contest is between the unname-

able and the narratable, the self as sovereign and the self as social. And there is no question of victory. Brontë is not trying to exclude, but to include, to preserve all the variations and levels of identity that come into play whenever the social act of authoring—or reading—a text takes place."[50] Brontë's engagement with these competing "readings" is also reflected in the tension between characterization and structure in her book, in which characterization gains an edge.

At first, this assertion might be surprising. Initially the architectonic design of *Wuthering Heights* seems to be composed of oppositions and repetitions so symmetrically arranged that, as one critic notes, the entire scheme appears to conform to a mathematical equation.[51] In fact, however, disproportions readily surface: for example, the failure of Edgar Linton to equal in characterizational presence his counterpart Heathcliff.[52] Grotesque Heathcliff, intrinsically more passionate and engaging his creator more passionately, deforms the structure of the novel. This deformity apparently suggests that beneath all modes of artificial order, artistic or social, lies a fundamental conflictive heterogeneity.

The violation of symmetry in *Wuthering Heights* occurs most significantly in the opposition and repetition characteristic of the narrative manner of the novel. This manner is repetitive insofar as Lockwood, the narrator, relates what Catherine's diary reveals to him or, more importantly, what Ellen Dean tells him, which is often what others tell her. Like the symmetry of character arrangement, such repetition quantifies in a way encouraging the reader, who might tend to associate quantification with verification, to credit at first what he or she is reading. Moreover, like the narrative-structure of *The Strange Case of Dr. Jekyll and Mr. Hyde*, that of *Wuthering Heights* communally includes the reader. The careful reader, however, finds Brontë's narrative-structure more vexing than reassuring, for the intimated promise of shared communal identity and of certain disclosure (truth) implied by narrative quantification/ verification remains uncertain, as flawed as is the fixed proportion implicit in the seeming symmetry of pedigree in the novel.

Nelly Dean's judgments constitute a "reading" of events. Once the credulity of her interpretations is challenged, the reader must wonder about the reliability of any of the sources of the account in the text. Like Lockwood, the careful reader remains skeptical about the structures of interpretation. Composing the outermost layer or frame of the narrative-structure of this novel, the reader must perform a personal act of evaluation.[53] More precisely, the reader must confront not only Nelly Dean's motivation but the reader's own desire to evaluate and to judge; for the ethical question of right or wrong options achieves no resolution in the symmetry of characterization or in the narrative-structure of the novel. The reader is thus forced to confront the puzzle of what has been related.

However, the reader's very terms (the novel implicitly admonishes) will tend to impose a forged order which, like the novel's near symmetry, will most likely prove unsuitable to the articulation of the reality and truth of the enigma of human community. By destabilizing structure and privileging characterization to reflect the communal inclusion of all levels of idiosyncratic identity, Brontë essentially abandons the reader to the inexplicable non-unitary nature of society. Although this maneuver implies that a large number of immediate ethical concerns must inevitably remain in a heterogeneous tension, the idea of community itself is ethically valued from Brontë's perspective as something very real.

So *Wuthering Heights* is a fascinatingly curious book. If this novel anticipates the function of narrative-structure as a signifier of communal ethos in the novels of some of her turn-of-the-century successors, it does so by conflicting the sort of value that narrative-structure would be given in their fiction (e. g., *The Strange Case of Dr. Jekyll and Mr. Hyde*). Brontë's destabilization of narrative-structure potentially alerts the reader to how ideas of social order are often too narrow or inaccurate, given the riddle of an inclusive polymorphous human community. Structure, therefore, is suspect, and in lieu of it Brontë focuses on character as the central mysterious cipher of the enigmatic social text. In this sense, *Wuthering Heights* anticipates the privileged place of characterization in modern novels, which similarly vex all structures of ethical judgment except the single ethos of individuality.

Assessing an ethical standard through in-depth characterization, even when as cogently managed as in George Eliot's novels, is difficult because such characterization necessitates an emphasis upon minutiae, upon a seemingly unstructured particularization of idiosyncratic thoughts and actions. There is the illusion of photographed situations or realistically rendered mental processes, both in some sense seemingly improvised, random, free. Characters thus presented "in the thick of it" also occlude the reader's perception of overview and of standards of ethics.[54] These characters, whatever the reader reads into them, do not necessarily or readily manifest authorially managed ethical concerns. On the contrary, in novels with "open forms" unresolved in meaning, characters tend to be exempt from a code typical of the conventional communal ethos of much Victorian fiction and (as in *Wuthering Heights*) to be presented in terms of a pathos implying the inherent value of self, particularly of the mental processes and of emotional intensities of the self as defined against others (society).[55] They often discover the emptiness or absence of values, search for them, or (as in the instance of D. H. Lawrence's fiction) impose new or renewed ones.

A Portrait of the Artist as a Young Man (1916), for example, depicts Stephen Dedalus, its protagonist, by means of the in-depth technique of the "stream of consciousness." Appropriately to Joyce's aesthetic intention, the author absents himself, not only avoiding authorial intrusions but also refusing to cue the reader in any way as to how to pass judgment on Stephen's thoughts and behavior. The penultimate sentence in the novel casts as much shadow as it might appear to shed light: "I go to encounter for the millionth time the reality of experience and to forge in the smithy of my soul the uncreated conscience of my race."[56] Just what is the tone of this remark, at once so weary ("for the millionth time") and so hyperbolic ("to forge in the smithy of my soul")? And in a related matter, do the religious allusions in the novel ramify or undercut the protagonist's thoughts? As the extensive critical debate over Joyce's alleged intentions in this novel indicates, the reader cannot finally determine whether Joyce presents his protagonist sympathetically or ironically, or both. Failure at this level for the reader certainly permits Stephen to live in all his complexity, which is artistically defensible. Nevertheless, we might observe without censorial implications, that what *A Portrait* and similar works gain in characterization they lose in structure —Joyce's management of epiphany is completely grounded on Stephen's perception[57]—and what they lose in structure, they lose in clarity of a standard of ethics frequently embodied in structure, especially as exemplified in the writings of Joyce's predecessors.

In contrast to Joyce's *Portrait,* Thomas Hardy's *Jude the Obscure* (1896) accentuates overall structure rather than in-depth characterization. In this novel, the narrative-structure of which we shall explore in Chapter 4, the force of plot-structure corresponds to fate, a fate of the endless repetition of human frustration and "the tragedy of unfulfilled aims,"[58] a fate reinforced by a failure in ethics by both church and state. Sue Bridehead initially rejects the values of both of these institutions. Appropriately, as a character she evinces a certain freedom at variance with the design of Hardy's plot-structure. Her thinking threatens to expand her presence in the novel beyond her role as the ethereal or intellectual opposite to the carnal Arabella, the other woman in Jude's life, a life divided between the dual claims of spirit and matter. This pressure against her structural fate as a foil (recalling the similar violation of symmetry in *Wuthering Heights*) in large measure accounts for her irritating vacillations and indecisions, for the confusion detectable in Hardy's less than certain management of her. As a "new woman" Sue strains for a freedom associated with in-depth fictional characterization; she contends not only with the predestining plot-structural fate of *Jude the Obscure* but also with Hardy's preference for a typology of character,[59] the mode of recapitulative (though often modernized or evolved) typical characterization most congenial to turn-of-the-century English novels disposed toward structure.

When in "Mr. Bennett and Mrs. Brown" Virginia Woolf indicts writers like Hardy for novels which remain incomplete, for requiring that "the reader should finish them, actively and practically, for himself,"[60] she has in mind primarily their use of typical characterization. But unwittingly she touches on an important, overlooked feature of typical characterization. The characters in a novel by Woolf appear to determine their own motives, and individual perspective emerges as the *sine qua non* of their creator's artistry. This effect does not actively engage the reader's imaginative reaction; it exhibits an integrity of character so complete that the reader is excluded and reduced to a fascinated voyeur. The interior flow of the thoughts and impressions of Woolf's "open" characters seem to invite intimacy, but in fact the reader serves only as witness; the reader is not particularly encouraged to think or act, nor can the reader interact with the characters' closed mental world sealed by the integrity of in-depth characterization. In other words, the reader of a novel by Woolf experiences the truth of Mrs. Ramsey's realization, in *To the Lighthouse* (1927), that each person possesses something so essentially private that it remains separate from another person, that finally each self is thoroughly Other to any self perceiving it. This observation precludes the possibility of the reader's genuine identification with Woolf's characters. The final exclusivity of Otherness in Woolf's fiction eventuates in an aesthetic enclosure (in which characterization supplants the dominance of structural design) so self-contained that the reader remains extraneous to it.

In contrast, the typical characterizations of novelists such as Hardy are subordinate to structure and consequently manifest much less individual freedom and motivation. Although these characters often possess idiosyncratic mannerisms, penetrating mental eccentricities are rare because they are "closed" representative types rather than "open" verisimilitudinous individuals. They are held as firmly as possible within a narrational point of view, and the reader is encouraged to identify with this "collective vision" comprised of a common culture, tradition, and custom informing the narrative-structure.

This identification of the reader with a collective narrative authority in these turn-of-the-century novels differs markedly from the stress of the later novelists on individualism. Like some of their Victorian predecessors, particularly George Eliot and George Meredith,[61] many turn-of-the-century novelists associate individualism of the sort to be favored by their successors with egotism, which they renounce through their insistence on a collective narrative viewpoint. Sometimes they explicitly remind the reader of his or her relation to the protagonist. *Anna of the Five Towns*, for instance, suggests a triadic interrelationship when its narrative voice remarks, "*Like most of us*, she lacked the high courage to grasp happiness boldly and without apprehension."[62] Here, among other instances, the reader is invited to "finish" (to use Woolf's word) the protagonist insofar as the typicality of characterization points toward the reader as someone whose individuality ought to be defined by and directed toward the identity of a shared human community still to be perfected.

In this sense, "closed" character types become open, in contrast to the so-called Modernists' "open" characters who are really closed to the reader.[63] In short, as Woolf noted, the reader of turn-of-the-century fiction must personally finish it. The reader is directed, as if in Schopenhauerian terms, to remark the noumenal (type) more than the phenomenal (individual) whenever the depth or interior of typical characters is absent. Drawn into this absence, and in some sense supplying the interior of typical characterization, the reader might internalize the lesson about the need to displace the egocentric perspective of the seemingly unique self with the collective perspective of the human community, the perspective many turn-of-the-century novelists objectified in narrative-structure.

H. G. Wells is representative in his stress on this collective perspective. Among his earliest writings is an essay (1895) arguing that "from the absolute point of view the universe is a perfectly rigid unalterable apparatus, entirely complete and finished."[64] Later in life Wells, influenced by Albert Einstein and Arthur Eddington, came to think of the finite universe as expanding infinitely, but he never abandoned the notion that from a hypothetical absolute point of view a "rigid" principle of order informs the universe and that the individual in this universe achieves genuine identity only in terms of a definition greater than the self: "consciousness of self . . . *is a serviceable synthetic illusion of continuity that holds the individual behaviour together,*" and "there is another life far greater than the individual life . . . the life of the species as a whole" evidencing a "collective will." Rather than total subordination of individuality or dogmatic individualism, Wells advocated "associated" individuals: "if a species survives, then it survives only by and through its individuals."[65] The individual was important to Wells, as to his turn-of-the-century peers generally, only in the context of a collective human meaning.

This notion, implying a hypothetical objective absolute view beyond individual subjectivity, similarly informs the preference for structure over in-depth characterization in the fiction of many turn-of-the-century novelists. Assuming something like a therapeutic role, they present each self as an inheritor of a definition dictated by the framework of a collective human identity. In *The Old Wives' Tale* representative characters are born, grow, age, and die in an inexorable series of parallel patterns; and the animal instinct in humanity to "go at it again and again" is, from the omniscient point of view of the novel, at once humorous and pitiable, and finally urges compassion from the reader.[66] Similarly, in Bennett's *Anna of the Five Towns* the narrator from beginning to end insists on prospects, a device borrowed from Romantic tradition; from these prospects the reader is directed to appreciate the narrator's sympathy for Anna, who is at once an individual and a type: "Look down into the valley from this terrace-height where love is kindling, embrace the whole smoke-girt amphitheatre in a glance, and it may be that you will suddenly comprehend the secret and superb significance of the vast Doing which goes forward below."[67] In John Galsworthy's *Forsyte Saga* (1906–22) typical characters are determined by (a satirized) social status, and this predestination is, from the narrative point of view of the novels, the measure of authorial concern with the evocation of greater humanitarian consciousness in the reader. In Wells's works exemplary characters like the protagonist of *The History of Mr. Polly* (1910) rebel against restrictive social and mental patterns to discover a

greater, more absolute principle of determination operating beyond humanity's desire for, as it were, a post-millennial utopia.

The turn-of-the-century novelists' emphasis, through
narrative-structure, on a larger, shared human meaning did not
ignore the concept of time. Time was a critical concern for
both sides in the debate defined by Woolf. For Woolf, Joyce, and
Dorothy Richardson time is psychologically registered. Main-
taining a view of time similar to Henri Bergson's idea of *durée*
and advancing both Henry James's technique of a "central intelligence" and the practice of other nineteenth-century novelists,[68] they conveyed time in their works through a stream of
impressions, thoughts, and images as filtered through a perceiving self. This degree of subjectivity seemed to many turn-of-
the-century novelists to be illusory, the product of egotistical
self-delusion. They tended to posit a larger, more objective "collective time" of which individuals generally remained ignorant
because a part cannot know the whole of which it is a part.
Turn-of-the-century writers, as a result, often held history in
high regard, a view epitomized in Wells's *Outline of History*
(1920).[69]

Wells could appreciate the use of perceiving intelligences in
fiction; he had in fact written a favorable and influential review of Joyce's *Portrait of the Artist as a Young Man*. But Wells
was sure that writers like Joyce defined time only in terms of
subjective perception; while accurate in a psychological sense,
this approach to time was inadequate when assessed from a collective human awareness. Always fascinated by a hypothetical
absolute viewpoint, Wells approached the relativity of human
perception not in terms of each individual but of the collective
species. In his novels after 1900 Wells aligned the mind of a
typical or exemplary character to the collective mind of *Homo
sapiens*, whose ever-expanding collective insight and destiny
were, for Wells, relative to any given moment in time or his-

tory to the paradoxical infinitely expanding finite universe. The human mind and the physical universe comprise, for Wells, two systems or frames of reference exemplifying the relativity of the four-dimensional continuum explained later by Einstein: "all the sequences of our individual and specific life are no more than a moving picture set in the frame of Relativity"; "the universe, the frame of life in space and time, expands with our knowledge, but it expands without apparent limit."[70] With this notion in mind Wells, after 1900, fashioned characters who are individuals, perceiving intelligences enjoying a delusive sense of personal freedom potentially fatal to the species; at the same time he made them *types* conforming to a fate infused with a potentiality for advancing the species toward some greater collective perfection.

For Wells, characters ought to be like the average person: at once unique and typical. As early as 1891, he had argued that in nature only approximate similarities occur. He repeated this idea as late as 1932, when he spoke of the implications of "a four-dimensional universe of unique events."[71] Wells was referring to the physical world, where the "freedom" of the random atom is our "fate."[72] He was focusing on how biology determines the individuality of a person.

However, Wells also saw the other side of this uniqueness. In 1895, he wrote: "individuals perish, living on only in their descendents, creatures of their body, separated pieces of their undying protoplasm: the type alone persists."[73] Some principle of order informs nature, which expresses itself in uniqueness. As late as 1942, Wells was still considering the paradoxical interaction of the unique and the typical. "When that space time continuum [defined by Einstein] is considered as a whole," he explained, classifications of individuals or species surrender distinctions and "merge into one another" so that finally there is "a Type specimen and a series of variations" of that type.[74]

An emphasis on type surfaces in Wells's fiction, and even comments in his *Experiment in Autobiography* (1934) reinforce his
ideas about types: "my individual story merges into the story of
the handicapped intelligence of the species, blundering heavily
towards the realization and handling of vast changes and still
vaster dangers and opportunities."[75]

The preference of many turn-of-the-century English novelists
for representative characters is again expressed by Wells in his
praise of Thomas Hardy's *Jude the Obscure* for its depiction of
a protagonist who is "at once an individual and a type."[76] In the
same year, again in the *Saturday Review*, he spoke of Ivan Turgenev's *Fathers and Sons* (1861) as a "novel of types": "The pecu-
liar characteristic of Turgenev's genius is the extraordinary way
in which he can make his characters typical, while at the same
time retaining their individuality"; "they are living, breathing
individuals, but individuals living under the full stress of this
great racial force or that."[77] It is a technique used by Charles
Dickens, whose Mr. Pickwick and Sam Weller adumbrate the
manner used by Wells in creating Kipps and Polly. The technique is also evident in the fiction of John Galsworthy, who
in apparent agreement with Wells argued, as late as 1927, that
"in the greatest fiction the characters . . . should sum up and
symbolize whole streaks of human nature," should be "not only
individuals but sections of mankind."[78]

This turn-of-the-century sense of proper characterization as
a combination of typicality and individuality echoes Engels and
Marx, who both adopted Hegel's view of the matter.[79] But the
source is much older than Hegel and finds particular emphasis
in Christian typological tradition. In this scheme a type refers to
a particular kind of symbol, a historical or actual person, place,
object, or event in the Old Testament foreshadowing its antitype, its fulfillment or explanation, equally real and historical,
in the New Testament. In most instances Christ is the antitype

revealing the secret symbolic meaning of the shadowy images or signs presented in the Old Testament. Typology comprises a closed world of symbols with (presumably) no room for interpretation, although the more liberal of the two patristic schools of typological thought allowed that the Old Testament types extend allegorically beyond Christ to include every Christian until the Second Coming.

Turn-of-the-century novelists probably knew little, if anything, about the intricacies of typological tradition. Regardless of their consciousness of the history of this cultural heritage, however, they appreciated certain allegorical features of literary art (as we saw in *The Picture of Dorian Gray*) that were, regardless of their knowledge, indebted to typological tradition. Moreover, even in its oldest modes typology persisted beyond the particular interest in it expressed by seventeenth-century Puritans, and these modes inform some examples of eighteenth- and nineteenth-century literature.[80] In early nineteenth-century America it informed Ralph Waldo Emerson's and Henry David Thoreau's attribution of a sacramentality to natural facts; in England it survived in the work of Thomas Carlyle and John Ruskin, who fused traditional biblical typology and the implications of modern science in an effort to translate fact into figure and thereby disclose a transcendental dimension in facts. Among the Victorians Gerard Manley Hopkins employed the typological system in his poetry and, before him, members of the early Pre-Raphaelite Brotherhood did likewise in their paintings, evoking through historical and contemporary details a sacred meaning to replace their sense of an exhausted cultural tradition.[81] Nor should we overlook George Eliot's *Adam Bede* (1859) or Thomas Hardy's *Tess of the D'Urbervilles* (1891) or his *Jude the Obscure*, to cite only three examples of nineteenth-century fiction in which typological manner conveys a timelessness indicative of the repetition of history.

For Hardy and other turn-of-the-century novelists like Stevenson, Wilde, Wells, and Galsworthy typical characterization was preferable to in-depth presentation because it suggested a viewpoint greater than individual subjective impressions. Belief in this larger perspective could be a premise for optimism (Galsworthy), pessimism (Hardy), aestheticism (Wilde), neutrality (Bennett), or ambiguity (Wells), but it functioned identically to the underlying scheme of typology and allegory. In fact, turn-of-the-century novelists' subordination of typical characters (supressing the claims of the self) to fictional structure (reflecting a larger communal viewpoint) corresponds, as we noted in our comments on Wilde, to the subordination of character to structural framework in allegory. Characters in turn-of-the-century novels often participate in a collective human identity, and the reader of this fiction is encouraged to identify with an encompassing narrative vision, an overview embodied in narrative-structure. Subordinated to structure, these typical characters serve the ethical message of this structure, and in this special sense they are "open" rather than "closed" because their representativeness and incompleteness (lack of in-depth presentation) invites the reader to become a sort of antitype, a further completion of their meaning and potentiality in relation to the human community. The reader ideally becomes a participant in the ethical demands of this fiction; concerning the typical characters of this fiction the reader, as Virginia Woolf remarked, must "finish them, actively and practically, for himself"—not only in the reader's experience of completing the text of the novel but also, ideally, in the reader's experience of living the text of life.

When such turn-of-the-century novelists as Stevenson, Wilde, Hardy, Wells, Bennett, and Galsworthy rendered characters according to this universalizing typological system and subordinated them to literary structure, they often intended to convey some ethical point of view. Ethical considerations remained paramount for many turn-of-the-century novelists in spite of the fact that they pondered cultural changes similar to those perceived by novelists like Joyce and Woolf. Turn-of-the-century novelists reflected on the implications of the ideas of Charles Darwin, Thomas Huxley, Herbert Spencer, Karl Marx, Arthur Schopenhauer, and Sir James Jeans; the rise of urbanization, of industrialization, of imperialism. They confronted the extremes of anarchism and aestheticism, and later the consequences of the First World War, Einsteinian time theory, Eddington's infinitely expanding universe, Planck's revision of classical physics, and the like. Such turn-of-the-century authors as Arnold Bennett, John Galsworthy, Rudyard Kipling, Thomas Hardy, H. G. Wells, Joseph Conrad, E. M. Forster, and the early G. K. Chesterton admitted the actuality of chance, fragmentation, and relativity in the phenomenal world, and many of them evinced a stoical attitude or an existential para-cultural alienation. A number of them, however, somehow also mustered a faith, admittedly an anxious faith often with a pessimistic undercurrent, in humanitarian ideals; others urged a profound, passive perspective of another sort. In short, many turn-of-the-century novelists expressed a faith in the possibility (however remote, potentially chimerical, or seemingly forlorn) of ethical reform (either Christian-humanist or Schopenhauerian, as we shall see) within human society.

And this fact is an important consideration to emphasize when we conclude with Frank Kermode that many turn-of-the-century authors seemed to resist the dismantling of fictional devices traditionally satisfying reader expectations, seemed to resist more modern technical innovations designed to reflect a changing time.[82] In fact, the seeming retention of easily recognized fictional conventions and the seeming reliance on a transparency of narrative by turn-of-the-century novelists can be deceptive, as Kermode detects in Conrad's *Under Western Eyes* (1911), which criticizes conventional ways of reading fiction even while its apparent respect for the authority of these conventions seems to invite commonplace expectations from its own readers. The newer writers were certainly more thorough and flamboyant in their technical innovations, but many of their predecessors also responded to some of the same turbulence of their time, responded subtly in their management of narrative-structure as an embodiment of their more evident (and perhaps old-fashioned) concern with ethics. Although these novelists realized that ethical considerations are dramatized through characterization, they also believed that these concerns became clear to the reader only when these characters reflected (as Hegel said they should) large social issues rather than mere individual idiosyncrasies and when these typical characters are placed within an informing structural framework. Just as in architecture structure directs the viewer's mental eye toward some totality of effect, structure in turn-of-the-century fiction (especially as exemplified by the "Edwardians," as defined by Woolf) guides the reader's mental eye toward some totality of ethical design.

In-Struction: Wells

This correlation of fictional structure and ethics by many turn-of-the-century English writers, implied in our observation about the inclusion of the reader in the narrative matrix of Kipling's "Phantom 'Rickshaw," is dramatically evident in another short story, "In the Abyss." This narrative by Wells, which seems on first appearance to be a tale of science fiction as slight as Kipling's ghost story had initially seemed, also exhibits a tension between structure and characterization.

Wells's "In the Abyss" is a relation with a message, but the perception of this instruction requires a sensitivity to the emergent narrative-structure of the story. Wells's story privileges this structure over characterization, a recurrent pattern in his early and late writings.[83] The privileging of structure in Wells's narrative conveys the ethical concern embodied in the tale.

At first encounter "In the Abyss" does not seem to evince many structural features. On the surface, in terms of its plot-structure, it appears to be a roughly linear account of Elstead's five-mile descent into the ocean; his discovery of a half-human, half-reptilian civilization; his near-death as a result of these creatures' worship of him; his accidental escape and return to the ship on the surface of the sea; and his second descent less than two months later, from which he never returns. But several times the reader is reminded that Elstead rendered his narrative "in disconnected fragments," a fact calling attention to the effort of the narrator to tell the story.[84] Moreover, the reader is especially reminded that the narrator, who finds it "impossible to re-tell it in [Elstead's] words" (p. 434), is presenting his text as a transitional narrative: one by no means complete and one nonjudgmental concerning the "verif[ication of] his strange story" of a suboceanic civilization (p. 444). The narrator certainly draws attention to himself when he refers to himself as "me" (p. 442), a "me" trying "to piece together the discrepant fragments of [Elstead's] story from the reminiscences of Commander Simmons, Weybridge, Steevens, Lindley, and the others" (p. 443). Indeed, given the fractional dialogue between two sailors at the opening of the story and the equally fractional discussion by other sailors while Elstead makes his first descent, and given in the account the abiding uncertainty concerning the veracity of Elstead's report, "In the Abyss" is, as a narrative, only *somewhat* more organized than are the many fragments of the testimony on which it is based. Whatever cohesiveness the story seems to possess derives from a self-conscious, tentative, negotiating voice, which guides the reader as best it can in a narrative that serves as an act of transition between the abyssal uncertainties of Elstead's disclosure and the stable meanings desired by the reader. This tripartite pattern of a narrative voice negotiating between Elstead and the reader parallels Wells's sense of the turn-of-the-century period as a "transition age"[85] between a past of apparent order and a future of uncertainty.

This subtle tripartite structure is reinforced in the tale by Wells's emphatic references to the depths of the sea and of the sky, between which resides humanity on earth's land surfaces, as if in a transitional state between the immensities of sea and sky. To stress humanity's intermediate position akin to that of the narrative voice and the turn of the century, Wells carefully, consistently (through the narrative voice) correlates sea and sky in the story. We are told that "the water above [Elstead's descending sphere] was as dark as the midnight sky" (p. 435), that "a hovering swarm of little fishes veered about and came towards him as a flight of starlings might do" (p. 437), and that shapes in the sea's depths were "as faint as the zodiacal light of an English summer evening" (p. 440). This correlation of sea and sky as abyssal immensities surrounding intermediate humanity is most pronounced in the narrator's explanation of how the suboceanic civilization would perceive our existence: "We should be known to them . . . as strange meteoric creatures, wont to fall catastrophically dead out of the mysterious blackness of their watery sky" (pp. 442–43).

This quotation reveals an allegorical trace in the "watery sky" analogy;[86] for through the correlation of the creature's watery sky and humanity's heavenly sky, the narrator of "In the Abyss" probes the question of how intermediary humanity, living in a transitional age between a nineteenth-century past and a twentieth-century future, will respond to the startling meteoric challenges likely to be encountered during the new century.

That the suboceanic creatures embody this allegorical trace is suggested not only by the association of their watery sky to our airy heavens and by the comparison of how their astonishment over something descending from above corresponds with our similar surprise were something alien to descend from our heavens, but also by references to their human features: such remarks as, in motion they "suggest . . . a walking man," "the vertical pitch of face gave it a most extraordinary resemblance to a human being," their forelimbs "caricatured the human hand," and these "man-like creatures" looked like "quasi human forms" (pp. 437–39). The connection between the creatures and humanity is hammered home when the narrator refers to the creatures as "descendents like ourselves of the great Theriomorpha of the New Red Sandstone age" (p. 442).

Because of this association, how these relatives of humanity react to Elstead's sudden appearance in their world is important to note. They respond by dragging his bathysphere to their undersea city, where they worship him as a god from above. They have, in short, responded to his presence by resorting to a conventional explanation; they have retreated into the past, with its protective superstitious beliefs, rather than confront the encounter with a mind open to the mysteries of creation.

This implicit tripartite scheme of past, present, and future, suggested in the creatures' reaction to Elstead, reinforces the narrator's effort to negotiate between Elstead and the reader in an age of transition. And from these developmental tripartite patterns emerges the instruction of "In the Abyss." The lesson of the story concerns humanity's transitional state during the turn-of-the-century period. Humanity can react to the future in a way similar to that of the manlike creatures, and like them live in an "everlasting night," a "perpetual night" (pp. 439,

442) of a mental darkness of superstition; or humanity can re-spond to the future by letting fresh encounters take "hold of [its] imagination," as Elstead's story affects Weybridge (p. 427), and by discerning these experiences with "eyes turned up in round wonder," as suggested by the two windows of Elstead's descend-ing bathysphere (p. 430). Imagination and wonder characterized Elstead's pursuit of the unknown, the abyss of mystery under-lying the universe. Elstead represents a response to the future in contrast to the reaction of the undersea creatures. His futuristic science[87] opposes their past-oriented superstition.

"In the Abyss," then, is a transitional text with an emergent narrative-structure comprised of tripartite patterns. The story exists in a "present" situated between the past and the future, superstition and science, the nineteenth century and the twen-tieth century. It even exists in a "present" situated between delusion and truth; for the accuracy of Elstead's report is left uncertain, something to be resolved in the future. Most signifi-cant, as narrative, "In the Abyss" exists in a "present" situated between Elstead and the reader; it improves upon the fragments related by Elstead, but it provides a still incomplete, unsynthe-sized, and nonjudgmental account, which ideally should be ad-vanced and refined by the reader in the future. This ideal reader will not react to the account with close-minded fear, skepti-cism, or superstitious belief, but with open-minded wonder, imagination, and scientific curiosity. In this way the narrative in-structs: its tripartite structural components incrementally or processively take shape (they in-struct) by expanding to in-clude the reader (Elstead > narrator > reader). This inclusion of the reader in a reiterated tripartite pattern conveys the message or instruction concerning humanity's options of frightened re-treat into the past and of bold, even possibly life-threatening advancement into the future. These are the ethical options,

Wells thought, that confront the turn-of-the-century reader of "In the Abyss."

That "In the Abyss" is a transitional—an incomplete, negotiating—text emphasizing perspective in a transitional age is less surprising when we note Wells's fondness for images of thresholds in his early short fiction. Windows in "Through a Window" (1895) and "The Plattner Story" (1896) figure importantly as a threshold of transition between two perspectives, as do doorways or passageways in "The Remarkable Case of Davidson's Eyes" (1895), "The Story of the Late Mr. Elvesham" (1896), "The Magic Shop" (1903), and "The Door in the Wall" (1906). Similar to the apparatus in "The Crystal Egg" (1897), through which a Martian views earthlings and a human sees Martians, "In the Abyss" is a transitional text stressing perspective. Specifically, it informs (and in-forms as) an emerging point of view in the ideal reader, who finds himself or herself included in the incremental tripartite narrative-structure of the story and who thereby finds himself or herself ethically instructed. The reader is instructed, first, to abandon the superstitions of the past and the desire for stable meanings such a retreat into the past signifies; second, to join in a tripartite fellowship with Elstead and the narrator, to refine the perception of Elstead and the narrator, and like them approach boldly, with imagination and a sense of wonder, the open-ended, even abyssal uncertainties of the future in the new century.

This reading of "In the Abyss" and my previous commentary on "The Phantom 'Rickshaw" have tried to demonstrate that certain turn-of-the-century English fiction is often concerned with communicating ethical notions, even sometimes in specifically popular genres of a seemingly slight nature; that in these works, as in fiction generally, a tension exists between characterization and structure; and that when these writings feature ethical considerations structure is usually privileged. The remainder of this book offers an empirical testing of these conclusions by way of in-depth readings of seven turn-of-the-century English novels. My experience with these works suggests that the correlation of fictional structure and ethics has been, however unacknowledged by literary critics, an abiding tradition in the history of the novel.

CHAPTER TWO

• •

•

Compassion and Fictional Structure:
Gissing and Bennett

In the last chapter we ranged through Victorian to early twentieth-century fiction in order to remark both the potentiality of fictional structure as a signifier of ethical vision and the limits of in-depth characterization as a communicator of ethical standards. In this chapter we leave behind such broad concerns and explore more extensively two turn-of-the-century novels. As a grid for observing how the authors of these two novels manage fictional structure as an indicator of ethical stance, we contrast two concepts of compassion that were available to these authors and other writers at the turn of the century: the Christian humanist and the Schopenhauerian. Arnold Bennett's *Anna of the Five Towns*, begun in 1896 and published in 1902, and George Gissing's *The Unclassed*, first published in 1884 and revised in 1895, are excellent examples of how their authors' understanding of one or the other of these two modes of compassion finds embodiment in the fictional structure of their work.[1]

Schopenhauer
and *The Unclassed*

Even in its revised form, *The Unclassed* is generally not regarded as one of Gissing's best novels. It is, however, as remarkable as Arnold Bennett declared it to be in 1899, when he was working on *Anna of the Five Towns*.[2] The chief difficulty with *The Unclassed* is not, as some critics have charged, the lack of a coherent attitude toward social problems,[3] for this peculiarity is a perennial crux in Gissing's fiction. The primary problem with this novel lies in its ending in a manner atypical for Gissing generally, and specifically not quite in accordance with the pessimistic tone and deterministic sequence of events in most of the book. The problem of the conclusion of *The Unclassed* is a subject we shall address shortly, but first we need to consider Gissing's Schopenhauerian view of life in this novel and of the role of the artist, particularly the nature of the artist's compassion.

It is important, however, to remember that German pessimism only reinforced Gissing's thinking at the time he worked on this novel, that this novel represents a tentative testing out of ideas, and that (like George Moore) Gissing did not consistently endorse German pessimism and its ideas throughout his career.[4] It is also important to note that although most of the explicit references to Schopenhauer in the first edition of *The Unclassed* were deleted from the revised version of 1895,[5] the influence of this German philosopher is still evident throughout and is more artistically embodied in the later edition.

The world depicted in *The Unclassed* is a Dantean inferno where people, engaged in the "miserable struggle" of existence, experience "ghastly torments" and "the pains of hell."[6] Even Osmond Waymark, Gissing's tentative spokesman in the novel,[7] suffers from a "dull half-conscious misery" resulting from hunger, bad health, and mental anguish: the "dark, foggy February mornings crushed him with a recurring misery which often drove him to the verge of mania" (U, p. 61). Several other characters in the novel cannot maintain their sanity. Bereft of a stoical attitude similar to Waymark's ironic sense of humanity's "wonderful faculty for accommodating [itself] to wretchedness" (U, p. 157), these "numberless struggling creatures . . . be their aspirations and capabilities what they might, must struggle vainly, agonise, and in the end despair" (U, p. 244). In the novel many of them contemplate or commit suicide, a last resort considered as well by Waymark and Ida Starr (U, p. 126), the protagonist of the book.

The Unclassed presents an extreme version of human existence. This world is described by a seemingly objective, frank, and amoral narrative voice; it is populated with people overwhelmed by a suicidal pessimism emanating from their experience of chance (U, pp. 166, 244) in lives so determined by impersonal forces that the meaning of existence eludes comprehension. In this world, freedom of choice, of volition, is an illusion engendered by each individual's manifestation of the primal will to live. Reality, as Waymark senses, is the "involuntary jigging" of humanity in a puppetlike dance (U, p. 78); it is the "sad fate half-foreseen" in Maud Enderby's face (U, p. 146). This perception of reality informs Waymark's detached endurance of his engagement to Maud, despite his cool preference for Ida: "fate had taken the future out of his hands; there was no longer even the appearance of choice" (U, p. 265).

At the center of Gissing's experimentation with Waymark's attitude and with "naturalistic" manner in *The Unclassed* is an adaptation of Schopenhauer's philosophy. Gissing's expert knowledge of German[8] and his particular attraction to Schopenhauer's thought[9] have been well documented. This recognition, however, has been restricted to critical discussions of the ideas in and themes of Gissing's novel. More significant to an appreciation of Gissing's artistry is the identification of Schopenhauer's influence on narrative manner and structure in *The Unclassed*. This book is especially appropriate to such an inquiry because it was the first novel Gissing wrote after he completed, in October 1882, "The Hope of Pessimism," an essay paraphrasing Schopenhauer's thought. Moreover, Waymark's reference to Schopenhauer (U, p. 214) is no random allusion in the novel, for it suggests an analogue which, in the light of "The Hope of Pessimism," provides a basis for an appreciation of the narrative manner and architectonic pattern of *The Unclassed*.

The opening paragraph of "The Hope of Pessimism" formulates a pivotal concept of Schopenhauer's thought that also informs the depiction of life in *The Unclassed:* "The mass of men are, for the greater portion of their time, under the domination of blind instinct, the instinct which whispers that they must cleave to life as to their dearest possession."[10] This fundamental egotism, Gissing argues, characterizes every type of human thought, including the agnostic humanism of late nineteenth-century Western culture, in which "the highest degree of civilization yet attained [coalesces] with the most flagrant social misery the world has ever seen" (HP, p. 88). Humanity's one hope resides in its capacity to recognize the hopelessness of existence through a "second birth of philosophical consciousness" yielding a "leaden-eyed despair"; this self-conscious despair permits the human mind to contemplate, and so mysteriously somehow to unwill, the instinct of life (HP, pp. 92–93). The effect of this kind of awareness corresponds to the renunciation advocated by Christianity and Buddhism, an apprehension of "the world [as] synonymous with evil" and as a "cenotaph of vanished hopes" (HP, pp. 88, 92). In this frame of mind, according to Schopenhauer and Gissing, one can glimpse the truth "that subject and object presuppose each other, and that if he would view this mutual relationship from without he must first transcend the conditions of his intelligence" (HP, p. 93). Such transcendence is impossible for the human mind, for the subject cannot know the object of which it is a part; the nature of phenomenal existence is "the pathos inherent in [this] struggle between the finite and the infinite" (HP, p. 94). Consciousness of this "pathos of the human lot" and of its attendant "cycles" is the most a human mind can achieve, and in the Schopenhauerian saint this consciousness produces a compassionate act of non-willing—the human mind's greatest approximation of free choice. This compassionate insight never effects changes in the fundamental "pathetic" condition of all life, which always intrinsically evinces a division between finite and infinite; it is merely the displacement of *"die Bejahung des Willens zum Leben,"* the assertion of the will to live, by *"die Verneinung des Willens,"* the denial of the will (HP, p. 91), an ascetic and pessimistic state of mind in which "the compassion which each man first feels for himself . . . extend[s] to his fellow-sufferers" (HP, p. 94). The most one can ever hope for is the worldwide attainment of this "sweetest sympathy" when humanity collectively refuses to reproduce itself, ceases to hope, and passively awaits its extinction.

Gissing, following Schopenhauer, identifies the chief expression of blind instinct as egotism, the assertion of will through individual personality (also a favorite subject of Gissing's predecessors). Typically, Abraham Woodstock, Ida's grandfather, possesses "from boyhood a powerful will [which] had borne him triumphantly over every difficulty" (U, p. 22). Similarly, Harriet Smales Casti, Ida Starr's antagonist, evinces a "restless, self-willed, discontented, sour-tempered querulous" disposition expressed in "self-willed habits" (U, p. 49). Ida too "match[es] her will" to that of Osmond, who "unconsciously display[s] something of that egoism which is inseparable from force of character" (U, pp. 39, 53). Of these characters Osmond is the most sensitive to the presence of a determining force—what Schopenhauer calls Will—behind the delusive activities of individual wills. His early experience of feeling "as though some voice were calling upon him to undertake a vaguely hazardous enterprise which yet he knew not the nature of" (U, p. 74) develops later into conscious belief in a determining force: "the doctrine of philosophical necessity, the idea of Fate, is with me an instinct. I know that I could not have acted otherwise than I did in any juncture of my life; I know that the future is beyond my control" (U, p. 215).

It is no accident that Waymark, the principal exponent of Schopenhauer's thought in *The Unclassed*, is an artist. Gissing shared Schopenhauer's view of the artist as the person most likely to achieve the "final triumph of mind, the highest reach of human mortality, the only hope of the destruction of egotism" (HP, p. 91): "The artistic mind, as Schopenhauer demonstrates, is *das reine Subject des Erkennens*, the subject contemplating the object without disturbing consciousness of self. In the mood of artistic contemplation the will is destroyed, self is eliminated, the world of phenomena resolves itself into pictures of absolute significance, and the heart rejoices itself before images of pure beauty" (HP, p. 95). In *The Unclassed* Waymark is this Schopenhauerian artist who believes his art to be determined by a life force and at the same time to be a vehicle of "liberating" self-awareness. For him art provides the self with contemplative moments when the self can briefly experience freedom from "the bondage of unsatisfiable longing" (U, p. 201) and so attain some sense of the transcendent Other of which every self is a small part. This concept of art informs Osmond's comment on the manner of his novel: its "direction may be imposed upon me; for all that, I understand why I pursue it" (U, p. 202). As he explains to Julian Casti, his friend, "I have come out of all that [misery], in proportion as my artistic self-consciousness has developed. For one thing, I am not so miserable as I was then, personally; then again, I have found my vocation. You know pretty well the phases I have passed through. Upon ranting radicalism followed a period of philosophical study. My philosophy, I have come to see was worth nothing; what philosophy is worth anything? It had its use for myself, however; it made me by degrees self-conscious and brought me to see that in art alone I could find full satisfaction" (U, pp. 201–2). Osmond's sense of the interrelationship of philosophy and art as well as his acknowledgment of the superiority of art to philosophy reflect Gissing's attitude in *The Unclassed*, an attitude derived from Schopenhauerian thought.

Osmond's devotion to art accounts for his attraction to Maud Enderby. As his "ideal personified" Maud characteristically speaks in a "low sad voice" indicating that her "life had in it so little joy" (U, pp. 72, 79, 215). Because "her very phrases had that musical fall which only associates itself with beautiful and honest thought," Maud strikes Osmond as "something higher than himself, a nature which he had to confess transcended the limits of his judgment, a soul with insight possibly for ever denied to himself" (U, p. 148). Osmond, the self-conscious Schopenhauerian artist, is attracted to Maud because of her intrinsic Schopenhauerian sensibility.

Their engagement is doomed, however; for whereas (like Osmond's) Maud's "soul . . . [is] that of an artist," (unlike Osmond's) her "aesthetic sensibilities [are] in perpetual conflict with her moral convictions" (U, p. 142). Maud is a devout Christian who at the end of the novel enters a convent. Her Christian renunciation (U, pp. 109, 292) is perceived by Osmond as an appropriate response to life because it expresses a "denial of the will to live," and this very compatibility of Christianity with modern pessimism leads Osmond to tell Maud, "I should have thought you had been studying Schopenhauer" (U, p. 214). But Maud has not quite arrived at Schopenhauerian nihilism, "the true successor of pure Christianity" (HP, p. 96). Since "the artist should be free from anything like moral prepossession" (U, p. 142), Maud is not destined to marry Osmond, the Schopenhauerian artist.

Osmond maintains that "the artist *ought* to be able to make material of his own sufferings, even while that suffering is at its height. To what other end does he suffer?" (U, p. 202). Unlike Maud, Osmond discovers no promise of spiritual redemption after death or of social amelioration in the world. When his friend, Julian Casti, says that Osmond's novel will do more good than a dozen religious societies, Osmond replies (suggesting too how the reader is to regard the implicit Marxist element in *The Unclassed* and reflecting, as we saw in Chapter 1, a view similar to that of decadents like Oscar Wilde), "There was a time when I might have written in this way with a declared social object. That is all gone by. I have no longer a spark of social enthusiasm. Art is all I now care for" (U, p. 201). Earlier, Osmond told Julian, "the novel of every-day life is getting worn out. We must dig deeper, get to untouched social strata"; so Osmond designs his novel "for men and women who like to look beneath the surface, and who understand that only as artistic material has human life any significance" (U, p. 112). For Waymark, as for Gissing and Schopenhauer, art discloses beauty, which alone temporarily relieves the self from its burden of "sin . . . the conscious enjoyment of life" (U, p. 214; cf. HP, p. 95).

Osmond and Maud perceive this beauty in art—Maud in Dante Gabriel Rossetti's poetry, Osmond in his novel—and both renounce the world. Their difference lies in the contrast between Maud's moral convictions and Osmond's amorality, and it lies even more significantly in the effect their respective attitudes have on the compassion each feels. Compassion is as central to Gissing's artistry in *The Unclassed* as it is important in Schopenhauer's philosophy, where it is the supreme positive principle of conduct. Paraphrasing Schopenhauer, Gissing writes: "The compassion which each man first feels for himself, let him extend to his fellow-sufferers" and yet refrain from hope (HP, p. 94). Compassion in this sense requires a larger view of human suffering than a person normally attains. This view reveals human misery to be intrinsic to existence (the will to live), meaningless, and beyond social reform. The compassion derived from this perspective comprises a state of mind, a profoundly sympathetic yet dispassionate awareness of the meaninglessness of all volition in a life determined by an impersonal force. It is an intellectual perception without emotional warmth or coldness, merely a non-self-pitying (and therefore mentally liberating) observation of one's identity with all other will-driven beings similarly caught in the futility of life: "Save our brother we [can]not, knowing not, alas, how to save ourselves; but our last word to him [should be] one of kindness" (HP, p. 95). This notion of compassion dictates the eventual failure of Maud's engagement to Osmond. Like Osmond, Maud perceives the world as a Dantean inferno, but her consequent compassion is aimed only at herself. She properly renounces the world, but her religious convictions direct her away from an agnostic skepticism and a detached compassion for her fellow-sufferers; her passionate self-pity after her mother's suicide urges her to seek her own salvation in a convent, a decision amounting to a withdrawal from life with an egotistical hope in her personal redemption. Maud dramatizes the perversity, in Gissing's and Schopenhauer's shared opinion (HP, p. 96), of the Christian mode of renunciation.

If Maud errs in her expression of compassion, Ida, who is explicitly contrasted to Maud (U, pp. 107–8), directs her compassion toward others, not out of an egotistical desire to reform society but merely because her modest philanthropic undertakings might lessen the misery of life for others. Because she was a homeless child who eventually had to prostitute herself to survive and who later was imprisoned on false charges, Ida feels an "instinctive sympathy" for the "unclassed" people who must not only suffer the anguish of the human condition in general but also specifically endure an unnecessary exacerbation of this state by the imposition of "social miseries" (U, pp. 280, 281). About the former Ida can do nothing for herself or for others; about the latter she can and does alleviate some of the societal denigration pointlessly inflicted upon the renters of her inherited properties: "She started with no theory and . . . had no very definite end in view. . . . [T]here was no danger of her being foolishly lavish in charity, when she could for[e]see with sympathy all the evil results which would ensue. . . . She knew that it would be impossible to remit the rent altogether, but at all events there was the power of reducing it, and this she did in many cases" (U, pp. 280–81). Ida especially attends to the children of the slum, for whom she unsentimentally creates little occasions of joy in their lives. She knows, however, that she cannot save them from their fate, just as she realizes that their "parents could not be reformed; at best they might be kept from that darkest depth of poverty which corrupts soul and body alike" (U, p. 281). Because her compassion is without theory or large purpose, because it is far from hopeful yet directed toward her fellow-sufferers, Ida is a better philosophical partner for Osmond than is Maud.

If Ida evinces a mode of compassion superior to Maud's, Osmond's compassion (in Schopenhauerian terms) surpasses Ida's. Osmond too is capable of selfless charity, as evidenced on the occasion when he gratuitously gives money to a desperate prostitute (U, p. 82). Later he expresses his compassion through art.

Compassion and Fictional Structure

As the Schopenhauerian artist eschewing any notion of his art as a manifestation of personal and social value, Osmond has no interest in the critical reception of his novel or in the probability that the book is "destined to bring the author neither fame nor fortune" (U, p. 278). For Waymark, as for Gissing and Schopenhauer, genuine art transcends such concerns; it conveys a vision of reality—the gulf between subjectively suffering humanity and the objectively impersonal Will, or life force. Art discloses the nihilistic reality "beneath the surface" of social phenomena and, in the subsequent dissolution of all human systems of value, implies "that only as artistic material has human life any significance" (U, p. 112).

In these terms, therefore, art ought to be realistic, not so much in the sense of a photographic reproduction of everyday human life but more particularly in the sense of a metaphysical awareness of the will to live, the reality so often disguised by social phenomena and human personality. Art is, as it were, the play within the play—an idea latent in Waymark's observation, "What a joke the word [freedom] must be to whoever is pulling the wires and making us poor puppets dance at his pleasure" (U, p. 78). Waymark's correlation of puppetry and human life cues the reader to associate Gissing's authorial management of his fictional characters with the delusive fiction of personal freedom and social distinction typical of the reader's world. This correspondence between the "reality" of the novelist's fiction and the fiction of the reader's usual sense of reality comprises the vision Waymark, Gissing, and Schopenhauer attribute to good art. This same "realistic" effect, correlating incidents in the reader's experience to episodes in the book being read, occurs when in a letter Waymark speaks of a change in his life: "So there ends another chapter. How many more to the end of the story?" (U, p. 78).[11] Similarly, in a conversation with

Osmond, Ida asks, "Well, are you thinking how you can make a book out of my story?"; to which Osmond replies, "I must wait for the end of it"; which in turn prompts Ida to retort, "Oh, you must invent one" (U, p. 136). Osmond indeed perceives Ida's life as a "story—a rather uncommon one, full of good situations" (U, p. 190).

Perhaps the cleverest instance of Gissing's covert identification of the puppetlike life of the reader and the contrived life of a fictional character—for the purpose of disclosing the reality behind the fiction of social rank and personality—occurs when Waymark's comment on his work echoes the title of the book in the reader's hands: "By some it [Waymark's novel] was *classed* with the 'unsavoury productions of the so-called naturalist school'" (U, p. 278; emphasis added). Whatever its classification, Waymark's book, like Gissing's novel, is antithetical to the late-Victorian penny weeklies, which Gissing condemns for perpetuating the very miseries their readers seek to escape (U, pp. 24, 99, 102). Gissing's sense of his own ideal reader points to someone who would duplicate Ida's response to Osmond's book: "It was horrible in many parts, but I was better for reading it" (U, p. 282)—"better" not in the sense of a subsequent urge to reform society but in the sense of an insight into the hopelessness of human existence. This insight might lead "sympathetic" readers to renounce the egotistical will to live and, like Ida and Osmond, in this way somehow reduce the misery of others or at least avoid making that misery worse. Essentially this insight inspires a stoical compassion, a detached caring devoid of emotion, sentimentality, or zeal for reform. This insight creates a frame of mind, a profound awareness and contemplative overview of the determined, immutable cyclic pathos of the human condition.

Structure in
The Unclassed

This mode of compassion informs the narrative-structure of *The Unclassed*, the first edition of which prompted one reviewer to remark on Gissing's need to make "an attentive study of the structural elements of fiction."[12] Encompassing the motions of the somewhat trite plot determining the interaction of the characters—and in the novel Waymark insists that we "look beneath the surface"—lies a subtle architectonic or narrative-structure pertinent to Gissing's detached compassionate overview of "the pathos of the human lot" (HP, p. 94). Gissing particularly emphasizes the pathos, rather than the tragedy, of the human condition.[13] In managing his characters, in making them as subordinate to fictional structure as humanity is subordinate to the predetermining Will of existence, Gissing does not present people tragically divided against themselves; nor do his characters evince an intrinsic dignity of heroic or tragic sort in their vain struggle for freedom or transcendence. Reflecting Schopenhauer's view of humanity, Gissing's characters experience a disjunction with the world; they suffer from an ever-frustrated and painful yearning for completion or satisfaction in a reality which always remains an elusively inaccessible and impersonal Other. Only death brings release from this "pathetic" condition, from assertion of the will to live, which is actualized in a repetitive rise-and-fall pattern constituting the human experience of the cyclic chance-dictated rhythm of conquest and submission. Just as Schopenhauer deems the circle to be the true symbol of nature,[14] Gissing stresses the cyclic (HP, p. 94), the repetitive pattern of human existence, from which each person is released only by death.

Gissing's perception of this "pathetic" condition of humanity accounts for the plot-structural rhythm of *The Unclassed*. As the characters of this novel interact, they experience a rise and fall of expectations. Ida Starr's experience is typical: her childhood security vanishes with the death of her mother, and she encounters the misery of life on the streets; from this low point her expectations reemerge when she meets Osmond Waymark, renounces prostitution, and takes a job as a laundress in an effort to regain even a trace of respectability; this optimistic state of mind is destroyed by her unjust imprisonment for theft; from this low point she rebuilds expectations about Osmond's affection for her; this hope is in turn dashed by Osmond's unavoidable failure to appear on the day of her release from prison; from this dejected state she again looks forward hopefully when Maud breaks her engagement to Osmond, who writes a letter which (at the conclusion of the novel) Ida reads with joy.

This rise-and-fall rhythm, reflecting the fundamental duality of life (the gulf between finite and infinite), is a feature of the plot-structure of *The Unclassed*. This pattern is contained within a still more encompassing circular or cyclic narrative-structure suggesting a still bleaker principle of reality: the overall unredeemable forlornness of humanity evident in each individual's experience of reality as a rise-and-fall rhythm. This more encompassing architectonic, the pattern of the omniscient narration, reduces further any possibility of a tragic dimension in the characters, who from the more remote viewpoint embodied in the narrative-structure seem truly (to apply Waymark's image) hopelessly puppetlike. In contrast to mimetic theatre, puppetry does not readily elicit the viewer's compassion; for in puppetry human dignity and capacity for volition—crucial elements of tragedy—are very distant, if not altogether banished. The compassion invited by puppetry is of a more detached sort than that engendered by mimetic drama, and it is precisely detached compassion that Gissing, in accord with

Schopenhauer's ideal, expresses through the narrative-structure of *The Unclassed:* an overarching design composed of a single event, reiterated by the omniscient narrator, that at once encompasses, reflects in large, and *reflects on* the rise-and-fall pattern of the plot-structural rhythms governing the protagonist's life.

This central episode occurs in the first paragraph of *The Unclassed,* where the reader is given an abrupt close-up view of a chaotic classroom filled with "screams and sobbings, hysterical cries for help" and an "ominous kind of moaning" (U, p. 5). This opening scene establishes the Dantean-inferno atmosphere maintained throughout the novel, an introduction *in medias res* particularly alarming because the sufferers are children. The result of Ida Starr's having gashed Harriet Smale's forehead with a slate board, this episode becomes a structural node through which the narrative loops three times. It is the occasion of Ida's "first great grief," when she is dismissed from school, witnesses the death of her mother, and undergoes subsequent misfortunes which eventually lead her to a life of prostitution.

The narrative of *The Unclassed* often evokes the reader's memory of this opening scene. Incidental instances include Philip O'Gree's threat to crown the schoolmaster for whom he works (U, p. 58); the time when, because Maud is struck in the head by a thrown book, Osmond spanks the schoolmaster's insufferable children, who, "yelling for help," flee their classroom (U, p. 75); and Maud's recollection of the initial classroom incident (U, p. 288). The two most significant and direct reminders of the opening episode occur midway in the novel, when much later in life Ida becomes Harriet's companion (U, p. 164), and Harriet successfully plots her revenge on Ida (U, pp. 178–85); and at the conclusion of the novel, when Ida completes her six-month prison term (the result of Harriet's false charges) and subsequently offers financial aid to her adversary, who rejects it "with insult" and shortly dies thereafter of a broken neck (U, p. 298).

Since *The Unclassed* is concerned more with Ida than with any other character, including Osmond (Gissing's provisional spokesman), it is appropriate that the critical event in her life, the opening classroom fracas, figures so prominently at the beginning, middle, and end of this novel. This symmetry, much more pronounced in the shortened, revised version of the novel, is reinforced by the facts that at the start of the book Ida is left destitute by the death of her mother on Christmas Eve and that at the end of the book Ida inherits wealth following the death of her grandfather on Christmas Eve. Similarly, whereas the opening episode presents children in distress, the final section of the novel emphasizes the occasional joy which Ida's restrained philanthropy provides for several children of the slums.

In their struggle for dominance Ida and Harriet express the will to live, as Schopenhauer and Gissing understood the life force. In the opening scene Ida is the victor, as Harriet lies prone; but this Pyrrhic victory results in Ida's subsequent tribulations. At midpoint in the narrative the contest is renewed, this time with Harriet the victor, as Ida is imprisoned; but this Pyrrhic victory causes Harriet's husband to desert her, which in turn exposes her to hard times. At the close of the novel Ida dominates, for she has inherited her grandfather's estate and is in the "superior" position of being able to aid ailing, destitute Harriet. The struggle ends only because Harriet dies. Equally important and more to Gissing's artistic purpose is the fact that whereas in the opening episode Ida dominates through an ego-gratifying anger, in the final encounter with Harriet, Ida dominates through an ego-denying compassion. Ida's detached compassion would not have curtailed the looping cycle of her encounters with Harriet—only the death of one of them could do that—but it would have lessened the intensity of those occasions because the force of the will to live would have been diminished.

Nevertheless, the conclusion of *The Unclassed* is curious. It may strike the reader as more optimistic than the rest of the novel would seem to support.[15] The ending is certainly atypical for Gissing, and very likely a more dire one appeared in the manuscript version of the novel. In fact the present ending might reflect George Meredith's insistence upon changes in the last part of the original version.[16] The ending of Meredith's *Diana of the Crossways* (1885) reveals a precisely similar tension and difficulty. Yet Gissing had to satisfy himself artistically as well, a probability which ought to encourage us to consider in what sense the ending is consistent with the rest of the story. The novel concludes:

Not many days after this, Ida, in London, received a letter addressed in a hand she knew well. There was a flush on her face as she began to read; but presently came a pallor of a sudden joy almost too great to be borne. The letter was a long one, containing the story of several years of the writer's life, related with unflinching sincerity, bad and good impartially set down, and all leading up to the words which danced in golden sunlight before her tear-dimmed eyes.

For an hour she sat alone, scarce moving. Yet it seemed to her that only a few minutes were allowed to pass before she took her pen and wrote. (U, p. 299)

This is a strange, oblique ending. On the one hand, it invites the reader to infer optimistically that Osmond and Ida will marry and be happy together. On the other hand, it avoids any direct statement to this effect. Moreover, the evasive indirection of "words which danced in golden sunlight before her tear-dimmed eyes" is countered by the explicit information that the

letter contained "the story of several years of the writer's life
. . . bad and good impartially set down, and all leading up" to
the undisclosed words. Gissing's manner here avoids any reference to marriage, while granting the reader the privilege of
inference; the undisclosed words might be only Osmond's report of his broken engagement to Maud. At the same time what
the narrative specifies in the letter recalls the pattern of Ida's
experience up to this point in the novel. In the specified passage
the contrapuntal words *bad* and *good, down* and *up*—whatever
their contextual disguise—recall the rise-and-fall design of all
the preceding episodes of the novel. In light of this intimation
of that pervasive pattern, the reader might on second thought
wonder whether the closing scene of the novel merely depicts
one more instance of the rise of Ida's expectations after a period
of sadness. The reader might further speculate that especially
given Waymark's restrained affection for Ida and his stoical acceptance of fate, the ascendance of Ida's hope in the final scene
might eventually be followed by an emotional fall, and so on as
long as she (or anyone) lives.

Moreover, the echo effect of the contrapuntal words pertaining to the specified passage in the letter is intensified by Ida's
expression of joy in "tear-dimmed eyes," an image remind-
ing the reader of the opening scene of the novel where Ida
and her schoolmates are crying. Although at the close of the
book Ida sheds tears of joy rather than tears of sorrow, both
actions express the will to live; the image of crying, recalling
the narrative-structural node of the novel, indirectly relates the
last episode to the opening scene. Such speculation by the reader
is reinforced by the recollection of Osmond's earlier remark to
Ida, that instead of killing themselves in despair, people ought
to "die at that moment—if it ever comes—when joy seems
supreme and stable. Life can give nothing further, and it has no
more hellish misery than disillusion following upon delight"

(U, pp. 125–26). The details of the plot of *The Unclassed* validate Osmond's observation, save perhaps the brief mention of O'Gree's successful business venture and of Ida's joy at the close of the book; both, however, are the product of chance and both are subject to decline given the context of (1) the rise-and-fall rhythm contained within the more pervasive unrelenting and cyclic repetition comprising the narrative-structure of the book and (2) the pathos of the human condition that structure defines.

All of these observations about the ending of *The Unclassed* are speculative. But they are as valid an inference as their opposite, the projection of marriage and happiness for Ida and Osmond. Although the conclusion of the novel remains evasive, there is no doubt that Ida's compassion resembles, more than does Maud's, the Schopenhauerian mode evinced by Osmond. Ida and Osmond belong to "the unclassed," not because they have both experienced the sort of poverty that reduces humans to subsocial status, but because their compassion exists outside the aspirations and value systems of societal and class consciousness. Insofar as is humanly possible their compassion, as manifested in her detached philanthropy and his disengaged artistry, is free from self-interest and from an equally egotistical zeal for social reform. Implicit in their stoical attitude is the Schopenhauerian recognition that in society the typical antagonism between egos actualizes the blind will to live underlying humanity's struggle, not (as in tragedy) with itself, but (as in pathos) with the world as an impersonal Other which fails to reflect for mankind any sense of human dignity, purpose, or hope. Ida and Osmond's profound but disinterested compassion parallels Gissing's narrative manner in *The Unclassed*, in which the author provisionally explores a Schopenhauerian response to life. Informed by the standard of Schopenhauerian compassion, Gissing's narrative presents life as "pathos" rather than as "tragedy," a distinction affecting the structure of his novel. That structure is not a spiral, which can (as in the writings of certain Romantics, the work of the Vortex artists before World War I, and in Wells's fiction of the 1930s)[17] signify hope in human progress. The narrative-structure of *The Unclassed* is a central event through which the omniscient narrative cyclically passes; it overarches the plot-structural rise-and-fall fluctuations which never modify the essentially "pathetic" condition of the structurally determined characters.

Structure in
Anna of the Five Towns

The influence of "Gissing . . . and the impersonal school" was noted by H. G. Wells in his ambivalent reaction to Bennett's *Anna of the Five Towns.*[18] One of Bennett's best novels, *Anna* correlates the disfigurement of the Bursley terrain by human industrialization, the degeneration of religious revivalism into mercenary ventures, the transformation of a religious person into a misanthropic miser, and the destruction of a young woman's yearning for something ideal by her eventual acceptance of a loveless marriage. Anna Tellwright, the protagonist of Bennett's novel, experiences the conversion of her "vague but intense longing skyward" into a stoical endurance of the fate "that a woman's life is always a renunciation."[19] Anna's destiny parallels the changes in the Bursley landscape and in the lives of its inhabitants; the inevitability of this correspondence imparts a pessimistic undertone to Bennett's novel, which manifests such other traits of Gissinglike "naturalism" as narrative frankness, amorality, and objectivity.

Bennett especially controls narrative objectivity. When, for example, Anna learns of Price's suicide, the result of his hopeless indebtedness to her, the narrative voice veers the reader's response away from sentiment by deflating Anna's sense of guilt: "She forgot that she had disliked the dead man, that he had always seemed to her mean, pietistic, and two-faced. She forgot that in pressing him for rent many months overdue she and her father had acted within their just rights—acted as Price himself would have acted in their place" (A, pp. 184–85). A similar restraint on the reader's emotional engagement, managed by narrative objectivity, occurs in the account of the death of Sarah Vodrey, the Prices' good-hearted and loyal housekeeper: "The next day [she] died—she who had never lived save in the fetters of slavery and fanaticism. After fifty years of ceaseless labour, she had gained the affection of one person, and enough money to pay for her own funeral" (A, p. 223).

The control of sentiment in such passages certainly augments their irony. Irony can be especially frigid in novels like those in the Gissing school identified by Wells; but Bennett avoided both icy irony and torrid sentimentality. He sought an objectivity between these extremes. While always ready to defend *Anna* against accusations of either sort, Bennett was particularly sensitive to the classification of his novel as an example of "the impersonal school," as Wells had remarked, and as lacking in emotion, as George Sand had noted. Responding to Sand, Bennett insisted, "The book is impassioned & emotional from beginning to end. Every character . . . is handled with intense sympathy."[20] Controlled management of emotion is, in fact, a significant feature of the narrative voice of Bennett's novels generally, and it is especially prominent in his *Old Wives' Tale*,[21] published in 1908, the year Bennett wrote in his journal: "I can and do look at suffering with scientific (artistic) coldness. I do not care, I am above it. But I want to hasten justice, for its own sake," so suffering "prompts me to support social reforms."[22] This dual reaction recalls Gissing's equally ambivalent position in *The Unclassed*, between detached observation of irremediable human suffering and implicit desire to alleviate this misery through social reform. But whereas Gissing's compassion is Schopenhauerian, at least in *The Unclassed*, Bennett's is Christian-humanist and Romantic.[23] Bennett cares while trying not to care too much.

In *Anna of the Five Towns* Bennett achieves this position partly by employing the "prospect" of Romantic convention. That is to say, the narrative voice directs the reader to some height where the reader can be "above it all" and attain a wider perspective than that of each of the individual characters in the novel. Of the five instances of this technique in *Anna*, the most significant occurs about midway in the book when the protagonist, vacationing on the Isle of Man, walks along "the high coast-range which stretches peak after peak," surmounts "the limit of habitation," and from this "prospect" experiences a vision of beauty momentarily satisfying her "intense longing skyward": "It was the loveliest sight her eyes had ever beheld, a panorama of pure beauty transcending all imagined visions. It overwhelmed her, thrilled her to the heart, this revelation of the loveliness of the world. Her thoughts . . . seemed to lose their pain. It was as if she had never been really unhappy, as if there was no real unhappiness on the whole earth" (A, pp. 155–57). This supreme moment, epitomizing Bennett's use of the "prospect," clarifies the implications of an early instance of this manner in the novel: "Look down into the valley from this terrace-height where love is kindling, embrace the whole smoke-girt amphitheatre in a glance, and it may be that you will suddenly comprehend the secret and superb significance of the vast Doing which goes forward below" (A, p. 25).

The secret is that life is composed of a dynamic dualism. Most evident is "the unending warfare of man and nature": "so ruthless is his havoc of her, so indomitable her ceaseless recuperation" (A, p. 25). Within this large encounter occur the many dualities (real or imagined) of human experience:

Compassion and Fictional Structure

life/death, spirit/body, joy/sorrow, love/hate, success/failure, expectation/disappointment, rise/fall, the beautiful/the ugly. Like Gissing in *The Unclassed*, Bennett in *Anna* emphasizes the rise-and-fall rhythm of these dualities of human existence, a condition no one can modify or escape. The narrative voice of *Anna* is "above it all" because it speaks of life from a "prospect" permitting identification with, at the same time as distance from, humanity. As Bennett wrote in his journal in 1896, the "essential characteristic of the really great novelist [is] a Christ-like all-embracing compassion";[24] Christ, who "fraternized with sinners" (A, p. 199), was at once of and above humanity, and so in Bennett's opinion is the ideal artist.

Although they both endorse compassionate objectivity in fictional narrative, Gissing's attitude is somewhat more detached than Bennett's. Whereas Gissing too recognized the applicability of certain characteristics of pure Christianity to artistic compassion, he believed that Schopenhauer's philosophy was the true successor of pure Christianity (HP, p. 96); herein lies the degree of difference between Gissing and Bennett concerning authorial compassion. Bennett is somewhat more ambivalent than Gissing about the hopelessness of the human condition.[25] Though they both para-culturally avoid any overt suggestion of significant social amelioration or of human adjustment to an increasing degeneration of the quality of life, Bennett evinces a vein of nostalgia implying that something vital in the human self has been stifled and that something valuable (at least potentially) in human culture has been lost. This trace of nostalgia, intimating a certain loss of human dignity, informs Bennett's equation of Christ and the artist. Whereas Gissing's compassion, derived from a philosophical overview of humanity, consists of a profoundly sympathetic yet detached observation of the *pathos* of the human condition, Bennett's compassion, derived from a para-cultural "prospect," consists of a nostalgically sympathetic yet ambivalently detached observation of the *tragedy* of the human condition. This difference between them is suggested in Bennett's citation of *The Nether World* (1889) as an example of Gissing's limitation as a novelist: "There are a dozen wistful tragedies in this one novel . . . but the dark grandeur which ought to have resulted from such an accumulation of effects is weakened by a too impartial diffusion of the author's imaginative power."[26]

So Bennett thought he had in his own work achieved a greater sense of tragedy than had Gissing; but that the degree of difference between Gissing's pathos and Bennett's tragedy is small is accidentally suggested in a complaint by D. H. Lawrence: "I hate Bennett's resignation. Tragedy ought really to be a great kick at misery. But *Anna of the Five Towns* seems like an acceptance."[27] Lawrence was responding to the elements of pathos in *Anna* that led Wells to associate the book with Gissing's novels. *Anna*, however, does not evince the degree of pathos evident in *The Unclassed* because Bennett's narrative veers somewhat more toward tragedy. This variance in degree of authorial compassion is a minor concern per se, but it led to a significant artistic difference between the architectonic designs of the narration of these two novels, a difference which accounts for the reader's sense of a certain elusive quality distinguishing *Anna* from *The Unclassed*. In *The Unclassed* Gissing's Schopenhauerian perception of the relentless and impersonal cycles of humanity's hopelessly miserable existence—the pathos of the human condition—is structurally expressed as a fixed nodal event through which the narrative loops three times. In *Anna* Bennett's ambivalent para-cultural view of how the intrinsic dualisms of existence frustrate the human self's innate yearning for something transcendent—the pathos and tragedy of the human condition—is structurally expressed as a triangle, along the three points of which the narrative rises and falls.[28]

Compassion and Fictional Structure

The narrative-structure of *Anna* is apparently designed after the model for tragic drama described by Gustav Freytag's *Technique of the Drama*.[29] Whether Bennett had firsthand knowledge of this work remains unknown at present; but given his perennial obsession with the dream of becoming a successful playwright, given his publication of plays before completing *Anna*, given his belief in 1901 that his "plays [would] make a market for [his] novels,"[30] and given his collaboration with H. G. Wells on a play during 1901–02,[31] Bennett most likely knew the main conclusions of Freytag's very popular book. Moreover, in his own remarks on playwrighting Bennett seems to have adapted Freytag's discussion of the triangular structure of tragic drama; he refers to "a pyramidal structure" when defining the interaction of playwright, actors, and audience.[32] In any event, whether originating from Freytag's direct or indirect influence, or from chance, the narrative-structure of *Anna* conforms to the pattern Freytag identified in tragic drama.

Specifically the narrative-structure of *Anna*, the macro-design in which the prospective omniscient narrator contains the events of the plot, exhibits the five-part pattern Freytag attributed to tragic drama: introduction, rise, climax, fall, and catastrophe. In *Anna* three events comprise, as it were, the points of this triangular structure. In contrast to Ida's "first great grief" in *The Unclassed*, the initial event in Anna's life occurs when she "realize[s] for the first time that she [is] loved"; "this was one of the three great tumultuous moments of her life" (A, p. 19). The events of the novel then "rise" until about midway in the book when the second major episode of Anna's life occurs: she accepts a proposal of marriage and has a "prospective" vision on the Isle of Man: "amid laughter and tears the brief and unique joy of Anna's life began" (A, p. 150). This emotional peak, what H. G. Wells described as "the top of the book,"[33] is followed by a "fall" in the narrative that ends with

Anna's climactic realization that she is not only lovable but also capable of loving, a painful discovery that "she loved another man" (A, p. 235) followed by her dutiful acceptance of a life of renunciation in a loveless marriage.

The "fall" and climax of *Anna* arrive somewhat more rapidly than the "rise" and emotional peak of the book, which feature disturbed several of Bennett's contemporaries.[34] Although he refuted this criticism publicly, Bennett on an earlier occasion in his journal confessed his own discontent with the swift ending of *Anna*;[35] and later in *Cupid and Commonsense* (1908), an adaptation of *Anna*, he even created a contrived and comic conclusion.[36] Nevertheless, the trouble Bennett had with the ending of *Anna* is not identical with the problem Gissing experienced with the revised ending of *The Unclassed*. Bennett's difficulty concerned pace, not consistency with structural configuration; for the conclusion of *Anna* conforms perfectly to the Freytagian triangle of tragic drama.

Anna's final "renunciation" (A, p. 235) differs from Ida's in *The Unclassed*. Ida appears to possess an innate character,[37] by means of which she preserves something akin to human dignity throughout her various tribulations. But she evinces the dignity of the stoical Schopenhauerian saint, who is largely disengaged from aspiration, expectation, and general concupiscence; whereas, in contrast, innately "simple" Anna evinces the dignity traditionally associated with a meaningful sacrifice of personal desire. Even if Anna's renunciation in fact serves no purpose, Bennett attributes to it an ironic poignancy derived from a nostalgic recollection of humanistic values. The reader senses not only the inevitable hopelessness of Anna's story but also at the same time the faint implication that in some ideal time, either in the lost past or in prospective human vision, Anna's life might have gone differently: not that she or anyone else in the novel could ever have transcended the dualities

of life, but that she could have been happier, could have lessened in the self the gap between yearning and fulfillment. In an
oblique way Anna's "intense longing skyward" (the dignity of
which is implicitly reinforced during her ecstatic moment on
the Isle of Man) grants heroic status to her acceptance of duty
in violation of her spirit, as if the pattern of her experience, in
some sense, corresponds to the "grim [and] . . . heroic" struggle
between mankind and nature (A, p. 25).

Whereas Bennett's Christian-humanist compassion treats
Anna's renunciation as a sacrifice, even though it occurs in
a world devoid of the values which would make her action
tragic, Gissing's Schopenhauerian compassion treats Ida's and
Osmond's renunciation merely as a stoical acceptance of the
pathos of human existence. Gissing and Bennett share a para-
cultural attitude toward human life, but Bennett is somewhat
more ambivalent and so cannot quite extricate himself from the
humanist heritage of the nineteenth century. Bennett's compassion might not exactly correspond to Kipling's sense of the
propriety of universal compassion (as we saw in Chapter 1), but
it grants humanity more intrinsic worth than does Gissing's
compassion; and this difference registers most prominently in
the narrative-structure of their novels. In *The Unclassed* the
omniscient narrator's perception of the pathos of the human
condition is expressed in his use of a single initial episode as
a fixed structural node through which the narrative cyclically
passes three times. Bennett's view of life accords with Gissing's
perception of pathos, but in *Anna of the Five Towns* his prospective omniscient narrator applies the rise-and-fall structure of
tragic drama to convey the faintest hint of tragedy while at the
same time indicating the absence of the religious or humanistic
value systems requisite to a tragic view of humanity. This variation in structure accounts for the different impressions these
two books give the reader, a significant variation resulting from

a relatively minor difference in authorial compassion. Whatever their differences, finally, both books are excellent turn-of-the-century examples of English fiction which privileges structure over characterization and which relies on this structure to convey ethical meaning, one feature of which concerns appropriate author/reader compassion.

CHAPTER THREE

De-Forming In-Struction:
Wells

H. G. Wells's novels *The Wonderful Visit* (1895) and *The Sea Lady* (1902) are even less popular now than they were when they first appeared. When they were published, both received mixed reviews, although their Swiftian satiric elements were generally appreciated; today critics barely mention these works in passing. The subjects of these romances—the arrival of an angel from another dimension, the appearance of a mermaid from beneath the sea—seem implausible and slight in spite of their allegorical nature. This impression of triviality, however, might be the result of authorial sleight of hand, for these novels are artistically more accomplished than critics have generally suspected. In fact, if these works are considered in terms of their similar structural technique, we can begin to appreciate better what Wells invested in them as aesthetic expression.[1]

In both romances structure, rather than characterization, is privileged, which is often the case in Wells's fiction, early and late, as we saw in our discussion of Wells's "In the Abyss" in Chapter 1. In *The Wonderful Visit* and *The Sea Lady* not only is structure privileged but, as our preceding commentary has argued, Wells's emphasis on structure is fundamentally informed by ethical concerns. Moreover, the one difference in authorial management of the otherwise similar structure of these two books signals a fluctuation in Wells's thought that finally highlights a difference in the philosophical ground of the two novels. Generated by Wells's ambivalence concerning the ability of mankind to save itself from a more-than-likely hopeless tendency toward self-destruction, this divergence in philosophical ground can be measured in terms of a difference between Christian-humanist empathy and Schopenhauerian compassion, a contrast similar to that detected in Chapter 2 between Gissing's *The Unclassed* and Bennett's *Anna of the Five Towns* (both of which Wells would read, also with ambivalence). Since this variance in ethos is embodied in fictional structure, which is the chief aesthetic feature of these two novels by Wells, careful attention to it will reveal something of the sophisticated artistry that can inform Wells's early writings even when they appear to be insubstantial.

Structure in
The Wonderful Visit

In *The Wonderful Visit* there are two references to Max Nordau, whose *Degeneration*, in English translation, saw seven impressions in 1895.[2] Nordau focuses on the turn of the nineteenth century as a time of degenerating transition from the established order of tradition to the dehumanizing chaos of passionate egotism. Although this view is not endorsed in *The Wonderful Visit*, Nordau is mentioned because the allusion to his views suggests that the fin de siècle period is indeed a time of transition, a time, however, when humanity faces an opportunity to choose between a decline of the kind described by

Nordau or an evolution of sensibility of the sort represented by the angel from another dimension of earthly possibility.

That humanity faces this critical choice is the message of *The Wonderful Visit* (as it was of "In the Abyss"), but it is not a message readily apparent in the plot-structure of the romance. This plot-structure culminates in the near-death of Sir John Gotch, who is mean-spirited; the passing away of Delia Hardy, who evinced a capacity for sympathy absent in her elite employers; the demise of the angel, who was increasingly succumbing to the poison of human passion; and the decease of Vicar Hillyer, who "never seemed happy" again during the few months he lived after the fire that destroyed the vicarage and killed both Delia and the angel (WV, p. 275). Indeed, the plot-structure of *The Wonderful Visit* expresses a pessimism similar to the dark view of life depicted in Wells's early science fiction.[3]

But *The Wonderful Visit* possesses a narrative-structure, one distinct from its plot-structure, that intimates the possibility of a development of human sensibility. This structure is not optimistic; rather, it disturbs the pessimistic pattern of the plot-structure by implicitly positing a human potentiality for positive change.[4] More subtle than the plot-structure, this narrative-structure is at first difficult to notice. It is the structure provided by the narrator, who consistently draws attention to himself and to the reader. The development of this structure implies the possibility of the evolution of the human mind by hinting at a correlation between, first, the narrator's effort to arrive at a more advanced, informed account of events than the fragments related to him and, second, the ideal reader's potential effort to arrive at a still more advanced, objective understanding of events beyond that of the narrator.

This narrative manner forms a tripartite pattern in which the narrator mediates between originally discordant accounts (principally rendered by Mrs. Mendham) and an exemplary sensitive reader. The pivotal importance of the narrator as a transitional figure struggling to organize data for the reader is emphasized through his numerous interruptions of his story, intrusions which draw attention to him and specifically to his function as a narrator.[5] "I am afraid it may be forgotten"; "I defy you to find another definition that will fit"; "I cannot tell you of the vision"; "as I think"; "for my own part I think" (WV, pp. 125, 127, 184, 185, 237): such intrusions, among many others in the text, indicate that the narrator is also a character in *The Wonderful Visit*, someone the reader might overlook if he or she tries to focus exclusively on the plot-structure of the account provisionally organized by the narrator. The narrator draws attention to himself not only in these relatively minor ways but also by enumerating the difficulties he encounters in trying to assemble the very story into which the engrossed reader is trying to escape. The narrator announces that he "is concerned with the facts of the case, and has neither the desire nor the confidence to explain them" (WV, p. 139); he at one point grumbles that he deserves a "resting place in this story" because he has "been hard at it, getting [the] story spread out" (WV, p. 177); and he admits that his account "is as much as anyone can tell you" (WV, p. 122), is as "far as [his] memory goes" (WV, p. 233). In short, the narrator is self-conscious and tentative, his voice negotiating between previous reporters and his readers. His voice (the text), bridging earlier accounts (the past) and the ideal thought-assembling reader (the future), symbolizes his (as well as Nordau's and Wells's) turn-of-the-century time, a crossroads, as it were, to be negotiated by the human race.

The narrator's self-conscious intrusions interrupt the reader's absorption in the plot-structure and prevent his or her escape into the illusion of this feature of the romance. These intrusions are a deformity in the plot-structure, a de-formity or breakdown of form in the plot-structure; but this deformity/de-formity gives life to an informing (message-bearing) narrative-structure for which the intrusions are in-forming (that which causes something to form). The average reader, Wells apparently hoped, would be disturbed by these interruptions, even as Hillyer is disturbed by the angel's revelations (WV, p. 203); but the exemplary reader will mentally process them and the discontent they arouse—an informing/in-forming process urged as well by the narrator's insistent use of the pronoun *you*. The direct address evident in the narrator's frequent use of this pronoun prevents the reader from merely vicariously experiencing the story; this direct address actually includes the reader, not in the story of the plot-structure, but in the narrator's laborious effort in the narrative-structure. "You may see it for yourself," he says in the first chapter (WV, p. 121). Elsewhere, he writes, "You would have been charmed at the couple could you have seen them"; "as the reader must admit"; "Dear Reader . . ." (WV, pp. 141, 178, 264). At another moment the narrator imagines the sort of review his "extravagant book" (WV, p. 131) might get from a wary reader. Indeed, the reader here is provoked into struggling with the text as much as the narrator has been wrestling with it. Like the narrator, the ideal reader becomes a character in the romance.

The presence of Mrs. Mendham and others (as sources of facts), of the narrator (as transitional organizer of the facts), and of the reader (as the next systematizer of the facts) forms a triad that vexes the dominance of the plot-structure, that vies with the importance of the plot-structure. The in-struction (the incremental pulling together) of this emerging narrative-structure (sources, narrator, readers) imparts an instruction or message: that the exemplary reader should further the story by learning from it, by contributing shape to it, and by passing it on as renewed insight to others in the future. This instruction/in-

struction of the narrative-structure expresses a tentative hope
in the possible evolutionary enlargement of a human sensibility that might rise above the blindness and egotism which in
the past and to date in the romance characterize human existence. This remains a tentative hope in *The Wonderful Visit*,
not a foregone conclusion; it counters, not necessarily defeats,
the pessimism of the plot-structure. The narrative-structure of
this romance conveys a message about a probable potentiality
within humanity to realize a higher self, symbolized by the
angel, a higher self Wells would later call a "collective will" (as
we saw in Chapter 1).

In the angel's realm, beings possess "wonderful imaginations"
(WV, p. 134), and it follows that for the narrator "the angel of
this story is the Angel of Art" (WV, p. 141).[6] The angel plays
beautiful music, which awakens in humans a sense of "longing,
a wish" (WV, p. 231), and a deep capacity to appreciate beauty:
"The study and the realities of life suddenly faded out of the
Vicar's eyes, grew thinner and thinner like a mist that dissolves
into air, and he and the Angel stood together on a pinnacle
of wrought music, about which glittering melodies circled and
vanished and reappeared. He was in the land of Beauty" (WV,
p. 184). The land of beauty glimpsed by Vicar Hillyer, whose
soul is quickened "to beauty and delight" by the angel (WV,
p. 252), is the place from which the angel has accidentally come,
a dimension of human possibility where "there is nothing but
Beauty" (WV, p. 138).

For humanity this dimension seems an imaginary realm, a
place "of beautiful dreams" (WV, p. 143). But for the angel it is
the human sphere that seems to be "the Land of Dreams" (WV,
p. 130). This application of the same image to both worlds implies that one is integratively related to the other and, therefore,
possibly one can be discarded for the other; for it is only a state
of mind (asleep, awake) that separates them. Perhaps humanity

will awaken from its present "dream ... that this narrow prison was the world" (WV, p. 258), where pain (of the sort dramatized by Gissing and Bennett too) "is the warp and woof of this life" (WV, p. 218).

The hope that imagination and beauty are available to humanity, if it awakens from one dream to another, is the message of the narrative-structure of *The Wonderful Visit*. The tripartite pattern of this structure, equating an age in transition (from the past to the future) to a tentative narrative voice transmitting past facts collected by others to an ideal future reader, is reinforced in the novel in a particularly pertinent passage designed to make readers especially self-aware of their act of reading and their role in the narrative-structure; in this passage readers learn that the human and angelic dimensions lay "somewhere close together" as "near as page to page of a book" (WV, p. 135). The very copy of *The Wonderful Visit* in the reader's hands here becomes an instructive/in-structive emblem of epochal and narrative transition from a past page to a future page of human life, including the reader's.

If the imagination and a sense of beauty are awakened (Wells's book suggests) mankind will evince a greater sympathy for fellow humans. When a little girl tears her hand on barbed wire, the angel is "sympathetic, comforting, inquisitive" (WV, p. 237). Through the angel's tutelage, too, Vicar Hillyer comes to realize that humanity has created (dreamed up) an "unsympathetic world" (WV, p. 258). And in this dream of a world, in fact, the angel receives no sympathy from most humans, who tend to regard him as a threat, as "an unhealthy influence" (WV, p. 249), as a maimed creature, or at best as a curiosity. The noteworthy exception is Delia, a servant girl who appreciates the imaginative beauty of the angel's music. When she tells the ailing angel (dying from the poison of the human dream life), "I am sorry for you, with all my heart" (WV, p. 261), she expresses an angelic sympathy of the sort that the exemplary reader will recognize as a model of human sensibility.

That Delia, a parlormaid, rather than her "betters," should serve as such a model is a violation of fictional convention that the narrator readily admits. He confesses that he must transgress the class stereotypes normally encountered in fiction: "I am painfully aware of the objectionable nature of my story here. I have even thought of willfully perverting the truth to propitiate the Lady Reader. But I could not. The story has been too much for me. I do the thing with my eyes open. Delia must remain what she really was—a servant-girl. I know that to give a mere servant-girl . . . the refined feelings of a human being, to present her as speaking anything but an intolerable confusion of aspirates, places me outside the pale of respectable writers" (WV, pp. 242–43). In fact his book has been doubly unconventional; if its heroine is a servant-girl who gives her life to save something precious for the angel, its hero is also not from the upper class, but rather is a beyond-class angel, who gives his life to save "lower-class" Delia.

Such violations of convention, especially as highlighted by narrative intrusions calling attention to these infractions, reinforce the reader's discomfort. Such breaches of fictional conventions are, like the narrator's self-conscious interruptions, a deformity de-forming the plot-structure. But these deformities contribute to an alternative informing/in-forming narrative-structure. Instructed by this in-structing narrative-structure, the ideal reader, aroused to thought by his or her inclusion in this pattern (vexing the plot-structure), will not retreat into the censorious past of convention or tradition. Rather, as suggested by an age and a narrative in transition, this implied reader might advance toward a more realized self in the future, a self awake to imagination, beauty, and active compassion. This exemplary reader will presumably further the instruction/in-struction of the text of *The Wonderful Visit*. A *hope* in the possibility of such a transformation in the reader informs/in-forms the narrative-structure of this novel, the same hope underlying the narrator's motivations, the "reasons [for writing] that will be more apparent as the story proceeds" (WV, p. 122). These reasons are never explicitly expressed, nor can they be found in the pessimistic plot-structure; these reasons are implicitly rendered in the hope embodied in the narrative-structure of the romance, a tentative hope in a vaguely possible human future of imagination, beauty, and active compassion.

Structure in
The Sea Lady

Although the serial version of *The Sea Lady* was published six years after the appearance of *The Wonderful Visit*, its internal chronology is set in 1899, only four years later than that of the earlier romance. That *The Sea Lady* might have been written several years before it was printed is an interesting speculation[7] since the novel is in so many ways similar to *The Wonderful Visit*. Like this earlier work, *The Sea Lady* concerns the sudden appearance of a mythological figure[8]—this time it is a mermaid rather than an angel—and satirizes the lack of imagination and wonder in those who encounter her. The plot-structure of this romance, like that of *The Wonderful Visit*, eventuates in death. Harry Chatteris, an initially unimaginative politician engaged to an equally prosaic woman representing the social elite, is infatuated by the mermaid, abandons his career and his fiancée, and fatally follows the mermaid into the sea. This plot-structure, like that of *The Wonderful Visit*, conveys a pessimistic view of the possibility of human reform.[9]

The Sea Lady also possesses a narrative-structure, a tripartite pattern of organization created by a narrative voice that, at least early in the book, seems to be identical to the one in *The Wonderful Visit*. This voice mediates between the reader and "broken facts," a "poor array of collected facts," facts "vague and incomplete."[10] This voice, like that in the earlier novel, draws attention to itself as it struggles to collect these facts from others and to impose a tentative order upon them during its relating of them to the reader. Both the self-consciousness of the narrator and the tentativeness of his narration are dramatized in such equivocating expressions as "I suppose," "as far as I have been able to piece it together," "I figure," "I believe," "I can't help imagining," "as much verisimilitude as I can give you," "I think," "I fancy," "I falter," "all I know is this much," and "of the end I can only guess and dream" (SL, pp. 323, 325, 326, 327, 329, 345, 350, 377, 475, 478).

There is, however, an important difference between the two romances in their focus on the reader. The reader is present in the later novel, as the narrator's self-conscious equivocations imply. But whereas in *The Wonderful Visit* the reader's presence is actively elicited, especially in the narrator's use of direct address, in *The Sea Lady* the reader's presence is more passively implied. This weaker presence of the reader in *The Sea Lady* is important to note, as we shall see, because it suggests that the instruction imparted by the in-struction of the emergent narrative-structure might not be precisely identical to that of *The Wonderful Visit*.

At first glance the message of the narrative-structure of the two romances seems to be the same. Like the angel in *The Wonderful Visit*, the mermaid in *The Sea Lady* symbolizes an ideal higher human self. Like the angel, the mermaid (Doris Thalassia Waters) possesses the ability to "alter . . . the values of things" (SL, p. 372) by seeming to hint at "something we never find in life. . . . Something we are always seeking" (SL, p. 447). Although the people around her generally fail to respond to her "mystery" and "wonder" (SL, p. 458), she (like the angel) can potentially activate the human imagination.[11] This faculty of the imagination is buried within humdrum human lives overshadowed by "the horrid modern spirit" (SL, p. 333), for which "the wonderful is utterly commonplace" and "only the familiar is really satisfying" (SL, pp. 336, 348). Even Adeline Glendower, Chatteris's prosaic fiancée, finds that her otherwise moribund "imagination was aroused" by the mermaid (SL, p. 347), and later, as she tries to come to terms with Chatteris's infatuation with the sea lady, she unwittingly but aptly remarks, "It is some mystery of the imagination that I cannot understand" (SL, p. 438). To Chatteris, Doris Waters is "like a picture . . . that's— imaginary" (SL, pp. 389–90); "it's a matter of the imagination" (SL, p. 399) for Chatteris, who by the end of the novel seems after all to have been "a man with rather a strong imagination" (SL, p. 439).

Reminiscent of *The Wonderful Visit*, this emphasis in *The Sea Lady* on imagination and a sense of wonder or beauty reinforces the narrator's sense that humanity is living in an "unwholesome little dream" (SL, p. 401). Perhaps mankind can awaken from this impoverished dream "to other dreams" (SL, p. 418) symbolized by Doris Waters's deep-sea world, where its inhabitants "drift . . . in dreams" (SL, p. 335). Precisely here, however, *The Sea Lady* differs markedly from *The Wonderful Visit*.

Whereas in the earlier story the reader is urged to complete more fully, in the text of self, the tentative, instructing/ in-structing text of the romance, in *The Sea Lady* the reader is less actively present, his or her potentiality for a more highly informed/in-formed self shadowed by doubt. Whereas in *The Wonderful Visit* the reader is urged to *act* heroically, like Delia and the angel, in the tentative hope that the better dream-world of the human imagination might be realizable, in *The*

Sea Lady the reader is at best invited to *contemplate* (not act to change) the limits of the dreamlike human condition. The uncertain hope present in the earlier story is absent from the later romance.[12]

This difference is indexed, in part, by allusions to the views of Nordau and Schopenhauer. In *The Wonderful Visit* Nordau's *Degeneration* is mentioned to emphasize that the reader's time is a period of transition when mankind can perhaps alter its state of mind from one dream to another, can perhaps choose between an apparent decline or a possible evolution of human sensibility. In *The Sea Lady* Schopenhauer's *The World as Will and Idea*, certainly as depressing as Nordau's book, is alluded to for the purpose of stressing the bleak fate of humanity imprisoned in a world which apparently cannot be transformed into a higher, more imaginative dream-reality. Like Nordau's volume, the English translation of Schopenhauer's work, first published in 1883, went though many printings during the turn of the century. The narrator's allusion to it in *The Sea Lady* is probably not a merely random one for Wells, who in *The Outline of History* (1927 edition) spoke of Schopenhauer's ideas as "profound and penetrating speculations" and who later adapted these ideas and gave them artistic embodiment in *Brynhild* (1937).[13] Just as the structure of *Brynhild* was influenced by Schopenhauerian thought, so was that of *The Sea Lady*.

According to Schopenhauer, reality, as mankind knows it, is really *Maya*, a place of illusions governed by a blind will evident in all life, but especially manifest in human egotistical striving for gratification. Even seemingly virtuous, charitable acts are really a mode of ego gratification, as indeed the mermaid suggests in her description of Adeline's behavior towards the poor: "In her heart she does not want their dreams to be happier, in her heart she has no passion for them, only her dream is that she should be prominently doing good, asserting herself, controlling their affairs amidst thanks and praise and blessings. . . . Vanity of vanities" (SL, p. 403). According to Schopenhauer, as we noted in Chapter 2, nothing can change this reality. The best we can hope for is a profound realization of the hopelessness of all existence, a recognition that might possibly result in a second birth of philosophical consciousness. This new awareness of the unmitigable pathos of human existence is the only sort of "action" available to humanity; for this insight can lead to a denial (all that is possible) of the will to live. This "act" of denial is expressed through a lack of interest in and detachment from the world, through a state of mind in which we compassionately contemplate (not try to change) the forlorn human condition and quietly await our own demise and the extinction of the human race. This Schopenhauerian *contemplative* compassion contrasts with the *active* sympathy for others of the Christian-humanist sort (in Delia and the angel) engendered by the tentative hope in *The Wonderful Visit*. This difference might explain why George Gissing, who (as we saw in Chapter 2) was at the time exploring the implications of Schopenhauerian compassion, admitted to Wells his dislike for *The Wonderful Visit*, but indicated his appreciation of *The Sea Lady*, about which he told Wells: "I do not pretend to interpret you with certainty; but what I *do* see is satisfying."[14]

The allusion to Schopenhauer's ideas occurs, significantly, in the last chapter and very near the end of *The Sea Lady*. The narrator reports that Chatteris's valet last saw his master sitting by and staring out an open window (an image of a desired imaginative escape). This "staring at nothing," the narrator says, is "indeed, as Schopenhauer observes in his crowning passage . . . the whole of human life" (SL, p. 472). That this remark is made by the narrator, rather than by some character in the romance, is important; it provides a key to why the narrative-structure in *The Sea Lady* differs in its implied resolution from that in *The Wonderful Visit*.

The narrator of *The Sea Lady* closes with the reader in contemplation of, not in encouraged active response to, the apparent futility of human existence. In lieu of the uncertain hope in *The Wonderful Visit* of a possible imaginative transformation of the world into a new dream-reality, there is in *The Sea Lady* only the "gentle ecstasy of death" (SL, p. 478). Chatteris's demise has none of the virtuous, heroic implications of the sacrificial death of Delia and the angel in the earlier romance. Chatteris's death follows logically from a sense of utter frustration and futility, symbolized in his defeated staring into a nothingness which cannot be transformed. This nothingness encompassing humanity is imaged by the narrator in the final paragraphs of the novel; mentioning "the margin of the softly breathing water" and "the extreme dark edge . . . of the sky" (SL, pp. 478, 479), the narrator provides two images which suggest that the edge of phenomena, of all creation, exists marginally between a sealike or skylike abyss of darkness. In fact the narrator's last words leave him, a policeman, and the reader staring, like Chatteris out his window, at nothing: "the interrogation of his [the policeman's] lantern must have gone out for a little way, a stain of faint pink curiosity upon the mysterious vast serenity of night" (SL, p. 479). With the narrator, the reader is left to contemplate (with implied Schopenhauerian compassion) the mystery of life (a faint stain of pink), the mystery of its complete futility, that our will-driven "blind" curiosity cannot transform or even fathom.

That the narrative-structure of *The Sea Lady* arrives at a Schopenhauerian pessimism which merges with the gloom of the plot-structure contrasts with how the fragile hope of the narrative-structure of *The Wonderful Visit* keeps that structure separate from the direness of the plot-structure. In both romances the narrative-structure deforms/de-forms the plot-structure, but in *The Sea Lady* the final alliance of these two structures results in a deformity/de-formity of the narrative-structure itself. In *The Sea Lady* the narrative-structure gets out of the control of the narrator, who consistently remarks his trouble in ordering his story (e.g., SL, p. 377); in contrast, the narrator of *The Wonderful Visit* gets his account into a transitional order in the hope of its further systemization and realization by his readers. The narrator of *The Sea Lady*, unlike the narrator of the earlier novel, cannot claim that his reasons for writing the book will become more evident as the story proceeds.

In *The Sea Lady* hope in some possible human action is intimated by the mermaid's symbolization of the capacity for empowerment by the imagination, by Chatteris's newly awakened desire to transform society (SL, p. 468), by the narrator's struggle to order the details of the story and communicate them to the reader, and by the example of a narrative-structure seemingly similar to that in *The Wonderful Visit*. But this intimation falls into silence as the narrator finally only contemplates the mystery of nothingness. Since his narrative-structure does not engender even a tenuous encouragement which would urge the reader to advance the text further in his or her self by acting hopefully for change, the direction of this structure is arrested, discontinued, finally interrupted, as the plot-structure triumphs. In fact, the narrative-structure fissures into two roughly equal parts: the first part (the seventy-two pages of the first five chapters) seems to assert a narrative-structure distinct from the plot-structure; the second part (the ninety-five pages of the next three chapters) deforms/de-forms this apparent integrity by subverting the emergent narrative-structure so that its instruction/in-struction reinforces the pessimistic message of the plot-structure and thereby leaves the reader reflective rather than urged to act.[15]

As a result of this reversal, the reader's vaguely felt expectations are frustrated, which in turn ideally should make the reader reflect upon his or her discontent—to contemplate. With the narrator at the end of his account, the exemplary reader will ponder the nihilistic outcome of life, as evidenced in Chatteris's suicide in spite of—or, more accurately, because of—the awakening of his imagination and sense of wonder by the sea lady. The narrator has told the story not in the hope of modifying human life, but with a contemplative Schopenhauerian compassion like that of the narrator of Herman Melville's "Bartleby, the Scrivener" (1853), when he says at the end of his narrative, "Ah, Bartleby! Ah, humanity!"[16] "Ah, Chatteris! Ah, humanity," the narrator of *The Sea Lady* might have thought at the end of his tale, as he and the reader stare at the dark sea and dark sky, at "the mysterious vast serenity of night," at abyssal nothingness.

In *The Sea Lady* and *The Wonderful Visit* we have two works which reflect an essentially abiding pessimism characteristic of much of Wells's early writing. In *The Wonderful Visit*, however, we see another side of Wells's mind that would become more pronounced in his later writings,[17] the side that fathered a tentative hope in the possibility that from a hypothetical absolute viewpoint (remarked in Chapter 1) life is not a Schopenhauerian void, but perhaps a dream of the Collective Will that can be transformed into higher modes of human existence. The force of these two countercurrents in Wells's mind registers so directly in the structure of *The Wonderful Visit* and *The Sea Lady* because structure, which is privileged over characterization in these two works, serves in fiction as a major embodiment of an author's philosophical and ethical beliefs. Read for their structural aesthetics, these two early romances by Wells can be better appreciated as engaging works of art more accomplished than their present neglect by literary critics would seem to suggest.

CHAPTER FOUR

Compassion, Fictional Structure, and the Reader: Hardy and Conrad

Given Thomas Hardy's and Joseph Conrad's apparent pessimism, the application of the concept of compassion to their work might seem eccentric; indeed, aside from the issue of pessimism, the very juxtaposition of Hardy and Conrad might at first seem odd.[1] However, even if the apparent sureness of narration in Hardy's *Jude the Obscure* (1896) seems to contrast with the less certain narration of Conrad's *Heart of Darkness* (1902), both of these novels can be read as corresponding literary representations of Schopenhauerian compassion. Their tentative exploration of this ethos is conducted primarily through Hardy's and Conrad's somewhat similar management of fictional structure in these two books.

Both these novels possess a spiral pattern of expanding and diminishing circles within circles. This thematically pertinent narrative design not only specifically revises the Romantic use of the spiral but also potentially involves the reader in the narrative process. The word *reader* here and in the following discussion, it is important to recall, refers to an implied reader, not necessarily to the actual post-Victorian reader. This ideal reader, suggested by certain clues in the texts reviewed in this chapter, participates in and contributes to the narrative-structure of *Jude the Obscure* and of *Heart of Darkness* in a manner even more artistically complex than in Stevenson's *Strange Case of Dr. Jekyll and Mr. Hyde*, Gissing's *Unclassed*, Bennett's *Anna of the Five Towns*, and Wells's *Wonderful Visit* and *Sea Lady*.

Schopenhauer
and *Jude the Obscure*

The critical debate concerning Hardy's pessimism is an old one dating from the late nineteenth century, when his novels first appeared. Beyond question, Hardy's fiction evinces a dark undercurrent, and the chief problem with the debate on this subject lies in the usually unacknowledged presumption that Hardy never vacillated in mood from work to work or, perhaps, never registered ambivalence in any given book.[2] In fact Hardy's pessimism varies in degree from book to book, with a tendency to darken after 1886 and then after 1900 to include some suggestion of social melioration.[3]

Hardy's pessimism originated from personal temperament and was reinforced by late-nineteenth-century scientific and philosophical thought attractive to this temperament. His views found support from many sources: the Bible, the Book of Common Prayer, Aeschylus, Sophocles (especially perhaps), Darwin, Huxley, Mill, Spencer, Taine, and Swinburne.[4] The work of the Greek tragedians and of Darwin are particularly gloomy when interpreted simply. Critics generally agree, too, that Schopenhauer's philosophy contributed importantly to Hardy's early dark perspective.

Explicit references to Schopenhauer occur in *The Woodlanders* (1887) and later in a passage not in the original version, but appearing in the first edition, of *Tess of the D'Urbervilles* (1891). Testimony comes as well from Eden Phillpotts, a fellow turn-of-the-century novelist who discussed Schopenhauer's ideas with Hardy, and from Hardy himself, when he remarked on his respect for Schopenhauer's thought.[5] Although Hardy's sensitivity to Schopenhauer is generally accepted by critics,[6] its extensiveness remains open to question, not only in terms of the usual difficulties encountered when trying to trace an author's sources, but also in terms of Hardy's specific attitudes and opinions. Possibly, for instance, Hardy was for a long time familiar only with the most basic principles of Schopenhauer's philosophy,[7] and much of what he grasped of this thought might have derived from Eduard von Hartmann, whose Schopenhauerian-influenced *Philosophy of the Unconscious* Hardy read in its third edition (1893).[8] How much of Schopenhauer's thought Hardy encountered firsthand or how well he understood what he read are finally moot issues. But Hardy's fascination with the philosopher's thought is demonstrable well beyond the fact that he owned a copy of Schopenhauer's *On the Fourfold Root of the Principle of Sufficient Reason and the Will in Nature* (English translation, 1887).[9]

Schopenhauer's presence is greatly evident and least adulterated in *Jude the Obscure*, the most pessimistic of Hardy's novels. The Schopenhauerian authority informing this novel was readily remarked in critical commentary on the book shortly after the turn of the century. Typical are Edward Wright's identification of Jude as Schopenhauer's perfidious lover and Harold Williams's response to the novel: "Not even Schopenhauer has made us feel so forcibly the continuity of human life in its generations."[10] Today, as well, critical discussions of *Jude* sometimes remind us of Schopenhauer's presence in the book, especially when they speculate about the primary influence on the epic features of the novel.[11]

Jude is replete with Schopenhauerian echoes. It emphasizes human "misery and depression,"[12] as did *The Unclassed* and as would *The Sea Lady*. Sue Bridehead tells Jude's son, "All is trouble, adversity and suffering" (JO, p. 406). Life is "Creation's groan," as Jude perceives it, "the grind of stern reality" consisting of, as it were, a hopeless "struggle against malignant stars" (JO, pp. 467, 473, 374). In the novel life is a gin, or trap, of heredity and social fate, a Darwinian predestination wherein (as Richard Phillotson remarks) "cruelty is the law pervading all nature and society; and we can't get out of it if we would" (JO, p. 389). The malignancy of this fate is not a personal antagonism directed against humanity; rather, it consists of the way people, like Jude, feel when facing the utter indifference of fate, especially when they necessarily fail to make rational sense of fate's purpose or of its apparent absence of design. In *Jude the Obscure* the principle of fate corresponds to Schopenhauer's concept of Will, the aimless force animating all creation and achieving fullest expression in the most highly evolved of species, mankind.[13]

Driving the plot of Hardy's novel is "a blind, amoral natural struggle, with consciousness an evolutionary accident leaving man as a creature who can think and feel and aspire but who is ruled by external and internal forces mostly beyond his control, forces indifferent to his wishes and values."[14] Humanity thinks, has ideas. This consciousness is mankind's greatest source of misery. The advent of human consciousness, according to Schopenhauer and Hardy, brought a painful self-awareness; and the self-aware person, Jude thinks, feels "as if he had awakened in hell. It *was* hell—'the hell of conscious failure'" (JO, p. 176).[15] This failure necessarily includes all aspirations, hopes, and dreams engendered by the ideas of a conscious mind. Consider Sue Bridehead's experience: "Vague and quaint imaginings had haunted Sue in the days when her intellect scintillated like a star, that the world resembled a stanza or melody composed in a dream; it was wonderfully excellent to the half-aroused intelligence, but hopelessly absurd to the full waking; that the First Cause worked automatically like a somnambulist, and not reflectively like a sage; that at the framing of the terrestrial conditions there seemed never to have been contemplated such a development of emotional perceptiveness among the creatures subject to these conditions as that reached by thinking and educated humanity" (JO, p. 417). The "full waking" of consciousness consists of the human mind's reflexive scrutiny of itself in the process of thought. The generation of ideas, a kind of animation reflective of phenomenal animation, disguises the aimless, nonrational Will, and these very ideas consequently contribute to the misery of "rational" humanity.[16] Unable to hold on to this conclusion, which might (in Schopenhauerian terms) allow her mind to turn Will against itself,[17] Sue lapses into the hell of conventional ideas.

For Schopenhauer, as for Hardy and Conrad, ideation is an illusion pervading all human behavior. Ideas are at once the result and the disguise of "the grind of stern reality" that always dashes these same ideas. This circular pattern constitutes the reality of Jude's life, which is chiefly characterized by the generation and frustration of idea-inspired aspirations. His is a loss by attrition, and near the end of his life he has nothing to replace what has been obliterated: "I am in a chaos of principles—groping in the dark—acting by instinct and not after example. Eight or nine years ago when I came here [to Christminster] first, I had a neat stock of fixed opinions, but they dropped away one by one; and the further I get the less sure I am" (JO, p. 399). Like Sue, however, Jude never quite arrives at a "full waking," that Schopenhauerian mode of contemplation in which the Will is meditatively turned against itself temporarily in the human mind, and when the human mind briefly transcends *Maya* (the illusion of phenomena).[18] Failing even at the end of his life to realize the malignancy of ideas per se, Jude says, "I felt I could do one thing if I had the opportunity. I could accumulate ideas, and impart them to others" (JO, p. 480). This remark is bitterly ironical, for Jude has indeed accumulated and disseminated ideas, has time and again suffered ideational illusion and disillusionment, in short has to the very end of his miserable life remained both victim and agent of the immanent Will.

Does Hardy's apparent distrust of ideation support Jude's belief that "there is something wrong somewhere in our social formulas" (JO, p. 399)? Does Hardy's novel indicate that social reform is possible through human self-control,[19] or that (as Arnold Bennett said about the book) social principles are beside the point,[20] or that social progress is at best ambiguous?[21] These are old questions for Hardy's critics. As early as 1918, the issue of the possibility of social reform in *Jude the Obscure* figures in critical estimations of Hardy's alleged artistic failure in the novel. Specifically, it is argued that the cosmic theory expressed in this book cannot support the fierce social protest also evident in the work.[22] Yet, twenty-two years later this same ostensible incongruity, viewed in conjunction with related disparities, is said to define "the secret of Hardy's success" as an artist.[23] The debate continues today, and the solution to this apparent incongruity can be found in the concept of Schopenhauerian compassion.

In fact, for Eden Phillpotts, a personal acquaintance of Hardy, Schopenhauerian compassion provides a key to Hardy's fiction: "What is his [Schopenhauer's] concept of 'Compassion' but an utterance of utmost beauty? Not to see all men in ourselves, but ourselves in all men, is an ideal as great as any. . . . Hardy and Schopenhauer share a deep and noble commiseration of his [mankind's] griefs and disillusionments, his vain expectations and blighted hopes. . . . Through life's frustrated dreams and desolate realities both great ones point a way of truth and clemency for all labouring under the manifold evils of conscious existence."[24] As we saw in Gissing's *Unclassed* (Chapter 2) and Wells's *Sea Lady* (Chapter 3), Schopenhauerian compassion is a state of mind, a profoundly sympathetic yet non-self-pitying disinterested awareness of the futility of all volition in a life determined by impersonal forces.[25] Schopenhauerian compassion requires a large perspective on life that discerns misery to be intrinsic to human existence (the will to live), to be meaningless, and to be beyond social reform. But even if social melioration offers no hope, it nonetheless can be considered necessary; for Schopenhauerian compassion requires the end of all human strife. So Jude is consistent with the Schopenhauerian implications of his story when he observes that something is wrong with social formulae. Social patterns presently compound human misery. Their revision will not improve the human lot in any progressive sense, but by curtailing artificially contrived miseries and by at least not adding to the human burden of conscious existence, social reform can express a universal human sympathy.

Renunciation, as Gissing made clear in *The Unclassed*, lies at the heart of this compassion. One must resist the demands of personality, particularly the principle of individuality.[26] In *Jude* Sue recognizes that the surrender of all ambition results in the most contentment one can experience in life (JO, p. 383). However, Sue's final declaration of "self-renunciation," of "sacrific[e] . . . on the altar of duty" (JO, pp. 419–20), is grounded on Christian and outdated social ideas, as was Maud Enderby's in *The Unclassed*. As such their renunciation is ill-conceived, not so much tragic as pathetic. Sue's "renunciation has nothing to

resonate *from* but expends its force in a great absorbent emptiness."[27] But if it is too self-centered, her instinctive attraction
to renunciation is, in Schopenhauerian terms, nonetheless correct.[28] Furthermore, her example is surpassed by that of Phillotson, who renounces (until the end, when Sue insists otherwise)
his conjugal rights, according to civil and religious authority,
only because he wishes to contribute nothing to Sue's plight.
Phillotson approaches the ideal of the compassionate Schopenhauerian saint. He does not speculate about progressive reform,
but by his humane behavior of compassionate renunciation implicitly revises social standards.

The issue of conjugal rights is important in the novel, for car-
dinal to the ideal renunciation of the Schopenhauerian saint is
a refusal to procreate. Nothing in *Jude the Obscure* supports
the will to live.[29] Everything in this work supports what Eden
Phillpotts designates as Hardy's Schopenhauerian "conviction
that it was better not to have lived than face the ordeal of life as
a conscious being."[30] In other words, like Jude, every human is
"born to ache a good deal before the fall of the curtain upon his
unnecessary life" (JO, p. 56). "It seemed such a terribly tragic
thing to bring beings into the world," Arabella is told by Sue,
whose sensitivity to the subject is later exacerbated by suicidal
Father Time's question about why people have children (JO, pp.
382, 407). The Schopenhauerian ideal of an eventual universal
human renunciation of life seems to inform Jude's comment
(concerning his son's murders and suicide) to Sue: "The doctor says there are such boys springing up amongst us—boys of
a sort unknown in the last generation—the outcome of new
views of life. They seem to see all its terrors before they are
old enough to have staying power to resist them. He says it is
the beginning of the coming universal wish not to live" (JO, pp.
410–11).[31] Although neither advocates suicide, Schopenhauer

and Hardy regard death as the only release from the misery of consciousness; and both regard a profound contemplative compassion, beyond religious dogma and social melioration, as an ideal state of mind anticipating the stillness of death.

Stasis suggests an ideal condition in *Jude the Obscure*, a novel so marked by incessant character movement that one recent critic complains, "There is too much fussy incident, too many comings and goings, concerning too many different towns."[32] This rebuke is understandable, if insensitive to Hardy's apparent aesthetic intentions; for the reader of *Jude* is indeed exposed to a disconcerting amount of incident and activity, particularly when the protagonist's "nomadic life" (JO, p. 379) is highlighted in the final two parts of the novel. The chief source of Jude's ceaseless motion lies in "the yearning of his heart to find something to anchor on, to cling to" (JO, p. 65). And here too for all humanity lies the origin of "the spirit of mental and social restlessness, that makes so many unhappy" (JO, p. 399). Neither nature nor society provides any holdfast; nor (as Sue comes to suspect) does any ascertainable First Cause behind nature and society become theologically or philosophically manifest to the "full waking" of human reason. The ceaseless animation of nature corresponds to the biological, social, and ideational motions of human life—a pervasive movement expressing Will and characterizing humanity's subjective experience of misery. This animation ceases only with death. When he dies, Jude lies "straight as an arrow" in the "motionless and quiet" air (JO, pp. 489, 490). His body has finally achieved peace from the futile ideas of its frustrated mind, and in death his body recalls the arrow Jude carved on a roadside marker: that ironically "static" emblem of the "moving" arrow of his ambition. Outside deceased Jude's bedroom the carnival of life goes on with its nearly frenetic activity.

Structure in
Jude the Obscure

Responding to this pervasive sense of movement in the novel, Ian Gregor remarks how *Jude* proceeds by a sequence of discrete moments having no inherent beginning or end—a processive sequence defying pattern.[33] In contrast to Gregor's point of view, J. Hillis Miller appreciates "a beautiful symmetrical design [in *Jude*], structured around harmonious repetitions and nearly patterned convergences."[34] The issue raised by Gregor and Miller—the question finally of structure in *Jude*—is a subject on which critics have disagreed as much and for as long as they have pondered Hardy's juxtaposition of universal pessimism and the need for social reform. Aware of Hardy's extensive architectural experience, early critics of this novel tended to expect a pronounced structure, and some thought the work was well designed, while others did not.[35] Edmund Gosse approached the novel as a rectilinear puzzle, the mathematical rigidity of which too much determined the characters' lives.[36] In a subsequent letter to Gosse, Hardy admitted that the plot of *Jude the Obscure* was "almost geometrically constructed," but he insisted upon the *almost* because "beyond a certain point, the characters necessitated it, and [he] simply let it come."[37] This comment is pertinent to our concern with the tension between fictional structure and characterization as well as with the privileging of structure over characterization in turn-of-the-century novels with a strong ethical position; and it is also pertinent specifically to the debate about structure in *Jude*. Hardy seems to defend both sides of this debate, at once supporting the suggestion of a rigid pattern of plot (as noted by Gosse and Miller) and the suggestion of a flow or motion of characters and incident seemingly bereft of any rigid design (as noted by Gregor).

Jude the Obscure certainly evinces patterns. The novel begins with the birth of Jude's aspiration and ends with the demise of his hopes. Moreover, each of the six parts of the novel repeats this rise-and-fall pattern.[38] This repetitive scheme corresponds to an emphasis in the novel on a parallelism, eventually a reverse parallelism, of events and of characters.[39] Even the conclusion of the novel consists of an inverted reflection of the beginning of the novel.[40] *Jude* possesses an iterative plot-structure, which becomes most pronounced at the end. Episodes and characters in the novel serve as mirror reflections of each other in a closed Schopenhauerian world in which generation after generation of humanity repeats the same "pathetic" rise-and-fall process of birth (hope) and death (despair).

This pattern informs Hardy's typological manner[41]—that is, as we noted in Chapter 1, his adaptation of the medieval biblical system identifying parallels between Old Testament types and New Testament antitypes as well as the Renaissance modification of this system designating correspondences between the figures of classical mythology and biblical personages. In *Jude the Obscure*, for instance, allusions to the "tragic doom" of "the house of Atreus" and "the house of Jeroboam" provide a context for "the tragedy of unfulfilled aims" (JO, pp. 350, 39) in the novel; a picture of Samson and Delilah (JO, p. 117) suggests a comparison between these Old Testament figures and Jude and Arabella; and Jude's sense of "what a poor Christ he made" (JO, p. 175) elicits associations between his and Jesus' suffering.[42] *Jude* abounds in such typological allusions because the self-contained mirrorlike reflections they imply reinforce the design of repetitive parallelism defining the closed Schopenhauerian world of the novel.

Implied-reader expectations generated by Hardy's system of parallelism, however, are frustrated because no character or event in the novel actually completes the typological analogy.

Rather, they (like mirror reflections) invert the source of the comparison. In this way something of the typological design is maintained, while at the same time the ideal reader senses a discontinuity, a perception equivalent to the narrator's sense of a "flaw in the terrestrial scheme" (JO, p. 55). This paradoxical appropriation and diminishment of typological design in *Jude the Obscure* reveal Hardy's acknowledgment (similar to Wilde's, which we remarked in Chapter 1) that in life, as in fiction, we seek, demand, and find design; but, for Hardy, in life, as in fiction, the *actual* phenomenal pattern we perceive disguises a still more pervasive *real* principle of animation evincing no system of order or purpose conceivable to the human mind. In the phenomenal world there are indeed natural and social cycles—the hours of the day, the seasons of the year, the episodes of history (including typological recurrences of a sort), the times of celebration in individual lives (births, weddings, funerals) and in communities (e. g., the Remembrance Games)—but these cycles consist of a *perceived* order, a pattern conscious beings discover or, more likely, posit in the closed world of which every person is a small, obscure part. Cycles are mirrorlike circular patterns in motion, and as such, Schopenhauer noted,[43] they symbolize the human experience of *Maya*, the deceit of phenomena.

So *Jude the Obscure* exhibits an intimated design of inverted parallelism. This *geometry*, to use Hardy's word, provides a mirror image of the reader's world, which presumably must be defined by a perceived pattern similar to that of the novel. Whatever is geometric in the design of *Jude* exists in the context of the closed world (the mirrorlike parallelism) of the necessary bounds of the text of the novel; and this context reflects the closed world (the inverted classical and biblical typology) of the necessary limits of the experience of the reader. Between the reader's perception and Jude's perception—that is to say, occurring at the periphery of the characters' world and of the reader's world—is the narrator's perception; and just as the narrative evidences a geometric plot-structure (while inversions challenge the very validity of the design they at once constitute and subvert), so too its narrator mediates between, and at the same time separates, the reader from Jude.

First, the narrator does not necessarily present Hardy's views. As J. Hillis Miller has noted: "In his fiction [Hardy] speaks not in his own voice but in that of a narrator he has invented" so that "the act of writing has an evasiveness or insulation which [Hardy] seems instinctively to have desired."[44] Second, the narrator is to some extent a character in the novel; he is not always detached, represents no absolute standard of value, shifts moods, becomes ambiguous, and expresses various opinions.[45] Third, as a result, the narrator is unreliable; at the periphery of his narrative,[46] he alternates between detachment from and involvement in Jude's experiences. These facts about the narrator potentially implicate the reader in the narrative process; for without a reliable narrator readers must look to themselves for judgment about and design in the narrative. This experience makes the reader somewhat more detached than the narrator without reducing that reader's share in the narrator's sympathy for Jude. In other words, the dynamic interaction of reader and text in this novel corresponds to the "motion" of natural and social cycles in Jude's life and of the alternation between detachment and sympathy in the narrative voice. This dynamic is cyclic or, to apply a more specifically geometric figure, circular. When the narrator seems detached, the reader tends to rely more on the account of Jude's perceptions; when the narrator seems less objective or seems to coalesce his view with Jude's, the reader looks to him- or herself. As if generating a series of expanding circles, the circumference of Jude's perceptions expands to the circumference of the narrator's viewpoint, which in turn expands to the still more encompassing circumference of the reader's observation. The reader becomes the outermost periphery of the text, as if at the edge of an expanding spiral— a position most pertinent to the narrative-structure of *Jude*.

The narrative-structure of this novel is based on the image of a dilating and contracting spiral, a rise and fall in the novel. The image of a spiral includes both the structural rigidity remarked by Gosse and Miller and the processive fluidity remarked by Gregor. Geometric rigidity defines the limits or the frame of the spiral, a frame which could be likened to an hourglass shape. This hourglass design also informs Hardy's *Return of the Native* (1878), in which it, at the level of plot-structure, embodies seven reversals or inversions.[47] In *Jude the Obscure* Sue and Jude similarly exchange positions. Coming from diverse points—he of Marygreen is religious, she of Christminster is skeptical—their lives intersect and then diverge—she at Marygreen becomes religious, he at Christminster becomes skeptical. Their final position vis-a-vis each other is a mirror reflection of their original positions, a plot-structure represented by an X, or hourglass design.

The hourglass configuration of the plot-structure of *Jude* represents the limits of fate, or Schopenhauerian Will. Within this delimiting hourglass configuration is a narrative-structure of the rise and fall of time's sand, the motion of all Will-animated phenomenal life, that can be diagrammed as a contracting and expanding spiral within this fated shape. As we have seen, rise-and-fall patterns occur as well in *Anna of the Five Towns* and *The Unclassed*. But there is a difference. Gissing's depiction of the rise and fall of his characters' expectations and Bennett's reliance on a rise-and-fall rhythm, both reflecting the fundamental and irreconcilable dualities of life as experienced by humanity, constitute the plot-structure of their novels, as does this pattern in Wells's *Tono-Bungay* (remarked in Chapter 1). Encompassing this plot-structure in both these novels is a narrative-structure—Gissing's omniscient narrator's use of a nodal episode reiterated thrice and Bennett's prospective narrator's use of the Freytagian triangle—to suggest inexorable patterns encompassing the rise-and-fall experiences of life. In both these novels the narrative-structure is a larger view on and, ironically, a larger version of the plot-structure. So, as Gissing, Bennett, and Hardy demonstrate, the pattern of rise and fall can inform either the plot-structure or the narrative-structure, or both, in a novel. In *Jude* Hardy associates this pattern principally with the narrative-structure of spiral-like dilation and contraction, a narrative-structure which (because Hardy's narrator is much less objective and omniscient than Gissing's or Bennett's) does not encompass but is contained within the hourglass-shaped plot-structure.

The disparate yet complementary expanding and contracting motions (like mirror images) of the narrative-structural spiral embody the laws of nature so insisted upon in *Jude*. Particularly insisted upon are the laws of "gravitation and germination" (JO, p. 191)—the centripetal force of spiral contraction and the centrifugal force of spiral expansion. Very early in the novel Jude experiences these two forces in a seemingly minor episode which actually adumbrates the pattern of everything to follow in his life. In this scene Jude shirks his duty to frighten birds, which creatures "seemed, like himself, to be living in a world which did not want them"; consequently, he is grabbed and spanked by Farmer Troutham: " 'Don't 'ee, sir—please don't 'ee!' cried the whirling child, as helpless under the centrifugal tendency of his person as a hooked fish swinging to land and beholding . . . [everything] going round and round him in an amazing circular race" (JO, pp. 53, 54). This incident results in Jude's movement (the centrifugal force of germination, growth) away from Marygreen; but it also forecasts Jude's numerous and increasingly wearying returns (the force of gravity, the centripetal force counteracting germination) to Marygreen throughout his life: in effect, "an amazing circular race."

Circularity is the chief image in *Jude the Obscure*, as in Schopenhauer's works.[48] Circularity informs the cyclic patterns of natural phenomena (e. g., "the planets in their courses" [JO, p. 68]) and of social behavior (e. g., the annual festivity days); it informs the typological repetition of human experience, especially the ceaseless repetition of rising centrifugal hope and falling centripetal despair within the limits of Fate or Will (the hourglass shape). A glimpse of this design occurs in the first chapter, when Jude, dejected over Phillotson's departure from Marygreen, looks into a well. He will return to this same well just before his death, and these early and late depressed visits to a "depression" in the earth are contrasted to his single encounter with Shaston (at precisely the middle of the novel), the "dream" city situated "on the summit of a steep and imposing scarp" (JO, p. 259): "The well into which he was looking was as ancient as the village itself, and from his present position appeared as a long circular perspective ending in a shrinking disk of quivering water at a distance of a hundred feet down" (JO, p. 49). Eleven-year-old Jude here stands, as it were, at the periphery of a spiral, or of a circle tapering downward. Pertinently, the well is "nearly in the centre of the little village" and is "the only relic of the local history that remained absolutely unchanged" (JO, p. 50). The well tapering downward symbolizes the spiral of time within the immutable hourglass of Fate or Will. In the well lies, as it were, the water of life from which (in Darwinian terms) all land creatures evolved, and the cycle of drawing life from water (moving the bucket upwardly along what seems to be an expanding circular wall) will eventuate in a return to this water (the fall of Jude's tear downwardly along what now seems to be a contracting circular wall, "into the depths of the well" [JO, p. 49]).

The image of Jude at the edge of a spiral appears again a few pages later, in the second chapter, when subsequent to his spanking by Farmer Troutham, Jude ponders life: "As you got older, and felt yourself to be at the centre of your time, and not at a point in its circumference, as you had felt when you were little, you were seized with a sort of shuddering, he perceived. All around you there seemed to be something glaring, garish, rattling, and the noises and glares hit upon the little cell called your life, and shook it, and warped it" (JO, p. 57). This thought, which seems more probably the narrator's than young Jude's, is partially correct; after all, Jude remains obscure, at the periphery of society. Life in the novel sometimes seems to be a centripetal contraction; but the preceding incident with Farmer Troutham, to which this later passage alludes, also indicates that life sometimes seems to be a centrifugal expansion. Both laws of nature exert themselves simultaneously and constitute the mutually antithetical, yet complementary, modes of intrinsic power (Will) governing the animation of all life. That being "at the centre" (in the passage on life in the second chapter) is as horrid as being at the circumference (in the passage on Jude's spanking in the second chapter) suggests the hopelessness of human life. Everyone is (as it were) always off-center and always longing for a holdfast "to anchor on, to cling to," even though the experience of being "at the centre" suggests there is no still-point other than death.

Consider Jude's two attempts at suicide that occur in the first and last parts of the novel. The account of the initial attempt, Jude's wish to die at the center of "a large round pond," emphasizes his search for a still-point in the midst of life's incessant circularity: "Jude put one foot on the edge of the ice, and then the other: it cracked under his weight, but this did not deter him. He ploughed his way inward to the centre, the ice making sharp noises as he went. When just about the middle he looked around him and gave a jump. The cracking repeated itself; but he did not go down. He jumped again, but the cracking had ceased. Jude went back to the edge, and stepped upon the ground" (JO, p. 116). In contrast, Jude's second attempt at the end of the novel is successful. By this time Sue, residing at Marygreen, has remarried Phillotson; Jude, residing at Christminster, has remarried Arabella. In one last frantic journey, Jude, already ill, goes out into the "deadly chill" of a "driving rain" in which "any sick man would have ventured out to almost certain death" (JO, pp. 467, 471). In this downpour he arrives at "the familiar well at Marygreen" (JO, p. 467), and after a brief, futile interview with Sue he returns to Christminster, where he admits to Arabella the suicidal intent behind his circular trip (JO, p. 472). This episode, which also involves water, parallels Jude's attempt to die in the frozen pond, to submerge himself in the apparent still-point of "the shrinking disk of quivering water" of the Marygreen well.

Time and again Jude centripetally returns to Marygreen, the place of his origin, the center of his existence from which his dreams and mistaken impressions of Christminster centrifugally radiate; and if Marygreen is in effect Jude's psychological and social center, then Christminster can be thought of as a place on an imaginary circumference around Marygreen. Ironically Jude does not die at Marygreen, but obscurely at its periphery. Christminster ought to have become a new center for him. When he first arrived at Christminster Jude seemed "to be encircled as it were with the breath and sentiment of the venerable city"; and although "for the present he was outside the gates of everything, colleges included[,] perhaps some day he would be inside" (JO, pp. 125, 133). Even near the end of his life (as Arabella remarks) Jude believes Christminster to be "a great centre of high and fearless thought" or (as he tells Sue) "the centre of the universe" (JO, pp. 383, 391). Christminster, the reader senses, ought to have become Jude's center, particularly given his eventual skepticism; but in this city he remains off-center, a peripherally displaced and obscure person. Also ironic is Sue's final residence at Marygreen. Sue ought to be the ideal emotional center of Jude's life; but with "unaccountable antipa-thies" (JO, p. 266), she is as elusive to him as is the still-point in the well. Sue never finds peace at Marygreen (JO, p. 491) be-cause this village lies on an imaginary circumference around Christminster, the place of her physical and intellectual origins.

Jude's and Sue's displacement to a psychological periphery leaves the reader off-center. That is, so many ironic reversals not only indicate but simultaneously efface the narrative design intimated by an unreliable narrator expressing both sympathy and detachment. These reversals finally abandon the reader on the outermost fringe of the text. The reader is left at the outer-most circumference of a narrative of spiral-like expansion from Jude's perspective, through the narrator's, to the reader's. The sympathetic and detached reader's final position at the edge of the narrative corresponds to Jude's position at the opening of the book, when he tearfully looks down the Marygreen well, and at the end of the book, when he, in a Job-like manner, enduringly looks inwardly upon himself toward rest, death. Throughout the novel the reader's expectations are aroused by the narrative, just as Jude's hopes have been evoked by Christminster. The reader's attempt to locate a philosophical, social, or aesthetic center or still-point in the novel is continually frustrated by numerous ironic reversals, by an unreliable narrator, and by the dimin-ishment of the narrative-structure (potentially message-laden) contained within the plot-structure, just as Jude's efforts to make Christminster the center of his life result only in baffling mirror inversions of everything. Finally the off-center reader is abandoned obscurely at the "phenomenal" edge of the text without any guidance concerning the many ambiguities of the narrative, just as obscure Jude dies at the "phenomenal" periphery of his dream without any definitive insight into the *reality* beneath the ambiguities of human existence. The reader's attention and expectation are centripetally attracted toward identification with Jude as the focal center of the text, only to be (through ironic reversals and unreliable narrative voice) centrifugally forced to the outermost circumference of the novel. In this way the reader becomes implicated in the controlling architectonics of *Jude the Obscure:* an intimated and ambiguous aesthetic design at once hourglass-rigid in its plot-structure and spiral-fluid in its narrative-structure.

This novel abounds in such ambiguities. Besides a structural pattern which is constructed and deconstructed, the work at once emanates and departs from the formula of the *Bildungsroman.*[49] Similarly, there is also the much-debated issue of whether the novel is in a formal sense a tragedy. Hardy speaks of the book as a "tragedy of unfulfilled aims" (JO, p. 39) and has the narrator allude to classical tragedy, particularly Aeschylus's *Oresteia* (JO, p. 350). In fact, the characters as well as the narrator so often use the word *tragedy* that, understandably, early reviews often praised[50] or condemned[51] *Jude* in comparison to Aristotelian standards of tragedy. Typical is D. H. Lawrence's rebuke that the characters in the novel are more pathetic than tragic.[52] Actually, as Arnold Bennett would do in *Anna of the Five Towns* and elsewhere, Hardy combined pathos and tragedy.[53]

The characters of *Jude* are tragic insofar as they are *somewhat* divided against themselves and *somewhat* evince an intrinsic dignity of a heroic sort in their struggle for a transcendent centering. But they also experience a permanent disjunction with the world. They suffer and (despite Jude's belief that life might have been better for him had he been born fifty years later [JO, p. 482]) they would have suffered at any stage of human history;[54] for in the Schopenhauerian terms of the novel, the ongoing misery of human consciousness is composed of an ever-frustrated absurd longing for completion (centering) in a cyclically repetitive phenomenal actuality of inversion that always remains an elusively inaccessible and impersonal Other. Herein lies the pathos of *Jude*, the pathos Hardy combines with an intimation of tragedy. And this pathos and tragedy are most notably commingled in the design of the novel. The point of intersection of the rigid hourglass plot-structure suggests the tragedy of missed opportunity; the rhythmically dilating/contracting spiral of the narrative-structure suggests the pathos of no possibility for any other outcome. Just as the tension between these two structures implicates the reader, who participates at the periphery by perceiving the simultaneous intimation and effacement of a structural still-point, so too with the tragic element in the novel. As James Kincaid has aptly noted about the sense of tragedy in this book: "We are continually being directed toward a pattern of action that is being inverted. It could be said, however, that the novel gains its power only by the discrepancy between these two patterns: the tragic pattern being completed in our minds and the ironic action insisted upon by the words on the page. The absence of tragedy thus becomes a presence."[55]

The tragic element finally remains primarily latent, or implied, in the text. It is always on the verge of emerging for the implied reader (at the periphery of the narration), whose expectations concerning tragedy have been raised only to be frustrated. This effect gives the reader an experience corresponding to the frustration encountered by Hardy's characters, who time and again seem on the verge of achieving some latent potentiality which finally always eludes them. In this way the reader becomes included in the Schopenhauerian world of the novel, the fixed, well-defined structural features of which in effect finally remain, frustratingly, only a potentiality. The reader comes to share Jude's reality, the experience of *Maya:* the ceaseless motion of phenomena intimating, while disguising a probable absence of, some ultimate causal design. There is no still-point of firm structure in the text for the reader, any more than Jude can locate a holdfast (ironically emblematized on the marker bearing his carved arrow) "to anchor on, to cling to." Because of numerous ironic reversals, an unreliable narrative voice, and a narrative-structure (intimating an ethical message) diminished by containment within the plot-structure, whatever is centripetally expectant in the reader's attempted closure with the text paradoxically must remain centrifugally detached for the reader abandoned at the outermost circumference of the spiral expansiveness (Jude > narrator > reader) of the narrative-structure of the novel. The mental "motion" in the reader of this simultaneous engagement and disengagement, empathy and detachment, apparently constitutes the primary aesthetic goal of Hardy's book: the urging of the reader toward a Schopenhauerian compassion, a profoundly sympathetic yet non-self-pitying, disinterested awareness of the futility of all volition in a life intrinsically miserable for all conscious beings, a life determined by an impersonal and aimless force (Will).[56]

This insight is achieved only momentarily in the reader's interaction with (perception of/construction of) the ever-emergent (or potential) narrative-structure of *Jude.* Just as this Schopenhauerian compassion is not the product of any system of thought—and Schopenhauer's thought is not systematic—so too Hardy's fiction remains "a series of seemings, or personal impressions" (JO, p. 39). As Hardy says, "A novel is an impression, not an argument."[57] At the periphery of *Jude,* the reader is given a glimpse from the periphery of life, where all conscious beings exist in phenomenal obscurity. This insight is identical to the one suggested by the reader's contemplation of margins and edges at the conclusion of *The Sea Lady* by Wells, who greatly admired *Jude* (see Chapter 1). This insight precisely corresponds to Schopenhauer's understanding of the aim of art: ideally, to make the perceiving mind less aware of itself as an individual entity, be still, and, without pleasure or pain, contemplate the what of the world.[58] And in this state, induced by the mind's *perception* of design in art (corresponding to humanity's *perception* of phenomenal patterns) the ideal reader (1) temporarily transcends the limitations of the self; (2) glimpses the absolute (if unknowable) significance beyond any imputed (albeit vehicular) pattern in natural, social, and artistic phenomena; and (3) now feels a profound compassion for every fellow human. This defines the apparent aim of Hardy's management of structure in *Jude the Obscure,* a remarkable experiment in Schopenhauerian aesthetics.

Schopenhauer and
The Heart of Darkness

Since Joseph Conrad, like Thomas Hardy, expressed a variety of moods and viewpoints throughout his literary career, no one of his works can be designated as more or less philosophically typical than another. In fact, reviewed collectively, Conrad's fiction may, as has been argued,[59] reveal three fairly distinct stages in his attitude toward human existence. Like Hardy, Conrad tried out ideas, different ideas in the same or different works, without necessarily endorsing any ideational system. Herein lies a distinct restriction on any discussion of influences on Conrad. Influences are present, but not systematically or with uniform intensity in any given work by Conrad, and not in such a way that they will yield some monolithic measure of all of his writings; nor is any given work simply the sum of the influences it evidences.

These cautionary remarks notwithstanding, *Heart of Darkness* may be approached in the light of Schopenhauerian thought. Even more than *Lord Jim*, composed during the same interval and equally privileging structure (as we shall see in Chapter 5), *Heart of Darkness* integrates theme, structure, and narrative voice in a mode of compassion for which an analogue exists in Schopenhauer's philosophy. Quite possibly *Heart*, like *Jude* in Hardy's canon, is Conrad's most pronounced experiment in Schopenhauerian aesthetics.

The degree of Schopenhauer's effect on Conrad's thought during the turn of the century is as difficult to gauge as it is in Hardy's. As usual, the irresolvable large questions about literary influence remain, difficulties worsened by Conrad's apparent delight in distorting and obscuring his sources.[60] Nevertheless, "of philosophy he had read a good deal," John Galsworthy said of Conrad, and "Schopenhauer used to bring him satisfaction."[61] Supporting this testimony by Conrad's personal acquaintance is a recent argument that the significant presence of Oriental thought in Conrad's writings was transmitted by Schopenhauer,[62] whose work is steeped in Eastern philosophy, especially Buddhism.

Reminiscent of the Schopenhauerian world of *The Unclassed*, *Jude the Obscure*, and (later) *The Sea Lady*, existence in *Heart of Darkness* is a Dantesque hell,[63] "gloomy circle[s] of some inferno" where "mangroves . . . seem . . . to writhe" and where people evince "attitudes of pain, abandonment, and despair."[64] Here resonates a "wail of mournful fear and utter despair," not only from the African aborigines but also (if in different ways) from Kurtz, who (as the epitome of civilization) is locked in "an intense and hopeless despair"; and from Marlow, who realizes that his "speech or [his] silence, indeed any action . . . would be a mere futility" (HD, pp. 47, 71, 39).

The phenomenal world of *Heart* is not substantial. It is as dreamlike as the Schopenhauerian world of Hardy's *Jude* and Wells's *Sea Lady*. "It seems to me I am trying to tell you a dream," Marlow says, "that commingling of absurdity, surprise, and bewilderment in a tremor of struggling revolt, that notion of being captured by the incredible which is of the very essence of dreams" (HD, pp. 27–28). Living in this dream-reality the characters of *Heart* see as if through a mist, gauze, or veil. The narrator compares the "mist on the Essex marshes" to "a gauzy and radiant fabric," and Marlow similarly speaks of human perception as "blurred by a creeping mist" (HD, pp. 4, 13). This prevalent mist is the veil of *Maya*, the Oriental notion adopted by Schopenhauer to describe the illusory nature of phenomenal existence. In this illusory, dreamlike phenomenal world everyone appears to be an inferno-like shadow or shade (HD, p. 78) and everything "seem[s] to belong to some sordid farce acted in front of a sinister back-cloth" (HD, p. 13).

Farcical life is "mere show" (HD, p. 29), Schopenhauer's *Vorstellung*. Since the human participants in this farce perceive each other only in terms of "show," they struggle (like the Company's chief accountant) to keep up appearances and they perpetuate the "sham . . . of all the appearances of success and power" (HD, pp. 18, 69). Appearance conveys humanity's social actuality, the mistlike veil behind which lies the isolated self animated by an incomprehensible life principle. As in *Lord Jim* too (Chapter 5), this "inner" reality is something "no other man can ever know. They can only see the mere show" (HD, p. 29). And similarly the "inner" reality of the phenomenal world remains unknowable, disguising *Vorstellung*. As Marlow says of his journey up the river, "When you have to attend . . . to the

mere incidents of the surface, the reality—the reality, I tell you
—fades. The inner truth is hidden" (HD, p. 34). The surface (*Vorstellung*, show) is all we can know of nature and of humanity.
Our perception is restricted to the mistlike veil of surface phenomena and our actions are limited to the "monkey tricks" or
the buffoonery of a "harlequin" (HD, pp. 34, 53)[65] performing in
"some sordid farce acted in front of a sinister back-cloth." Life
is a "jig" driving away silence or void (HD, p. 30).

Farce, monkey tricks, jigging, traveling—all suggest (as in
Jude too) that human life is motion, animation, a harlequinesque *danse macabre*, "the merry dance of death and trade"
(HD, p. 14).[66] Observing how the Africans "howled and leaped,
and spun, and made horrid faces," Marlow is struck by "their
humanity" and by his "kinship with this wild and passionate uproar" (HD, pp. 36–37). Motion makes up the blurry veil
which is phenomenal existence. This motion is the essence of
Maya, the illusion of phenomena animated by Will, not only
in the world but particularly in the human mind. The human
mind *moves* by the mental activity of conscious thought. Consciousness and the ideas it engenders are, in the Schopenhauerian terms we remarked earlier, the products of the actualization of Will. For Schopenhauer *Vorstellung* means both "show"
and "idea," and like the deceit of appearances, the ideational
show of human consciousness constitutes the intrinsic misery
of human existence.

Kurtz's anguish arises from his consciousness. He is a man
with ideas and with a sense of duty, somewhat like Jude's, to further these ideas (HD, pp. 60–70). In *Heart of Darkness* ideas are
as illusive as are natural and social phenomena, and typically (in
Marlow's judgment)[67] the *ideals* of Western civilization, especially when predicated on chimerical *ideas* about progress, are
ostensibly "what redeems" Kurtz, as the agent of civilization
(HD, p. 7). Assessing his experience of the encounter of the ideas

of Western civilization and human behavior in the African jungle, Marlow concludes, "It was as unreal as everything else—as the philanthropic pretense of the whole concern, as their talk, as their government, as their show of work" (HD, p. 25). *Show:* all human activity of mind (talk) and body (work) constitutes *Vorstellung;* and above all else, Marlow suggests, imperialism epitomizes the lie which is *Maya* (illusory life), "that mysterious arrangement of merciless logic for a futile purpose" (HD, p. 71). This latter observation by Marlow itself deceives; for the signified meaning of its words ("merciless logic," "futile purpose") pretends to mean even while in this particular combination they cannot signify, or make sense, to the rational mind. The words of this statement cancel each other as they confront our rational expectations; but the experience of the process, or deceptive animation, of the words of this statement conveys an insight into the "show" of all human mental and physical activity, insight into the reality that we all "live in the midst of the incomprehensible" (HD, p. 6).

In *Heart of Darkness* conscious beings—that is to say, humans partaking of and contributing to the motion of phenomena—can find no refuge from the misery intrinsic to their existence. Even when Marlow dreamily senses that he has returned "to the earliest beginnings of the world," where he perceives "the edge of a colossal jungle" and, as it were, "peep[s] over the edge" of animated phenomena, he discovers a "stillness of life [that] did not in the least resemble a peace. It was the stillness of an implacable force brooding over an inscrutable intention" (HD, pp. 34, 13, 72). Death is the only exit from the inherent frustration and misery of conscious existence, and this is perhaps why to Marlow the shrunken heads on poles seem to smile (HD, p. 58).

Short of death, Marlow's example suggests, the best one can do is reduce his or her harlequinesque role in the farce of life's

danse macabre by attaining an attitude similar to that of the
Buddha. The Buddha tableau, as William Bysshe Stein has remarked, appears at the beginning, middle, and end of *Heart
of Darkness*, an arrangement calling attention to itself. Stein,
however, misses the Schopenhauerian analogue for this image.
Marlow's lotus posture does not symbolize his "detachment
from the conditions, the victories, and the vicissitudes of time";
the novella nowhere intimates that Marlow is "qualified to
enter nirvana" but "remains in the world to work for the salvation of all people."[68] On the contrary, Marlow reveals his
compulsive attachment to the subject of his narrative, an attachment held in uneasy dialectic with the distancing manner of
a somewhat detached narrator. Within the aesthetic phenomena of *Heart of Darkness* Marlow's disposition simulates what
he once glimpsed at the less animated edge of his perception:
a "stillness of life [that does] not resemble a peace. It [is] the
stillness of an implacable force brooding over an inscrutable
intention." In body as in mind, Marlow's "ascetic aspect . . .
with arms dropped, the palms of hands outwards" (HD, p. 3),
evidences the disposition of the Schopenhauerian saint, whose
particular mode of compassion keeps him at the periphery of
human existence, at once subjectively involved in and somewhat objectively detached from the misery of conscious life.

Although in his narrative Marlow indicates that he is "not
particularly tender" (HD, p. 16), throughout his account he exhibits concern for others, compassion.[69] His early efforts to be
compassionate suggest a Christian-humanist point of view, but
eventually he arrives at a Schopenhauerian perspective. However hopeless the gesture—and with Schopenhauerian hind-
sight Marlow sees the irony—he offers a dying African a biscuit
(HD, p. 18). A corresponding sensibility informs his recollection of a deceased helmsman: "I missed my late helmsman
awfully—I missed him even while his body was still lying in

the pilot-house. Perhaps you will think it passing strange, this regret for a savage who was no more account than a grain of sand in a black Sahara. Well, don't you see, he had done something, he had steered; for months I had him at my back—a help —an instrument. It was a kind of partnership" (HD, pp. 51–52). Here Marlow discloses not only a metaphor for his sense of the absence of any ontological steerage in creation—an echo of his earlier remark that "there was nothing [of Company power] behind" him (HD, p. 28); he also, simply, discloses a compassionate recognition of the essential bond among all humans, at whatever level of social or intellectual development. This sympathetic identity accounts as well for—again, however futile it proves to be—his tug on the string of the boat's whistle to disperse the aborigines on the shore before his passengers could get their rifles ready for the "jolly lark" of pointlessly shooting the Africans (HD, p. 69); and, however ironic it remains, it accounts for his "lie" to Kurtz's intended at the end of the narrative. This "lie"—that Kurtz's final words were her name—is also the truth, for the illusion in which she lives typifies for Marlow "the horror" Kurtz discovers at the heart of illusory civilization,[70] the horror of ontological absence at the core of *Vorstellung*. But the ironic coding of Marlow's reply to Kurtz's fiancée emanates from Marlow's evolved Schopenhauerian compassion. His "lie" does not contribute pointlessly to another's misery and at the same time it does not falsify the truth;[71] in short, it epitomizes the Schopenhauerian saint's engagement in (the compassionate "lie") and detachment from (the ironic truth) human existence.

Marlow's final mode of compassion, like the narrator's in *The Unclassed*, in *The Sea Lady*, in *Jude the Obscure*, and in *Lord Jim*, does not implicitly advocate some ideal of social reform, as if a change of this sort could really improve the human condition. In *Heart of Darkness*, as we shall see in *Lord Jim* too, Marlow's small compassionate actions amount to little more than nothing. Marlow's experience simply indicts civilization, especially as manifested in the extension of misery through the imperialistic mission of bringing self-awareness to unself-conscious natives. He indicts civilization as a masquerade of the horror which *is* human consciousness, a masquerade which (in the guise of a "civilized" progress) augments human misery by implementing a social context always likely to "provoke the most charitable of saints into a kick" (HD, p. 25). Marlow compassionately dissents. With a few minor, feeble Christian-humanist efforts to relieve human suffering behind him, Marlow quietly opts for a posture of passivity, a disposition offering him no safety from the world and composed only of a profound detached compassion for humanity.

This compassion informs Marlow's refusal to judge Kurtz, whom he sympathetically believes to have "suffered too much" (HD, p. 57). Marlow's comments were carefully edited by Conrad with the intention of minimizing, if not completely eliminating, a judgmental vocabulary: for example, the *Blackwood's Magazine* version lacks the word *atrocious*, which in Conrad's manuscript Marlow uses to describe the Company manager's thoughts; and the book version lacks the words *of cruelty and greed*, which in the magazine version Marlow uses to refer to Kurtz's "amazing tale."[72] Marlow does not feel superior to anyone in the story, not even to his African helmsman. He tries not to judge (especially in Conrad's final version of the text), for he compassionately recognizes the bond uniting all suffering humanity. But also, significantly, he is remote.

This two-sided disposition characterizes the motivation of his concern with Jim in *Lord Jim* and his visit to Kurtz's fiancée in *Heart:* "Curiosity? Yes; and also some other feeling perhaps" (HD, p. 74). This remark is as deftly worded as is his "lie" to Kurtz's intended. Curiosity implies a voyeuristic detachment from her plight, but it also simultaneously suggests Marlow's inability to escape, to become completely disengaged from life. Just as Jude is immersed in "something glaring, garish, rattling," Marlow is attracted to the glitter of phenomena and the glitter of Kurtz's life, a glitter evident in the eyes of Kurtz's fiancée.[73] The vaguely referred-to "other feeling" paradoxically becomes the opposite of, respectively, detachment and engagement. This combination, as we have seen, precisely defines the nature of Marlow's "lie," that deceiving act (supporting the "show" of life) which is also an expression of truth-telling, disengaged compassion (intimating the horror behind *Vorstellung*). And this combination precisely defines Marlow's narrative manner in *Heart of Darkness*. As he relates his story in the darkness, he sits detachedly still, like a Buddha; but he speaks, uses language and its ideational content, and so participates in the animation which is *Maya*.[74] Like Kurtz, Marlow is "very little more than a voice" (HD, p. 49). As evidenced in the "lie" he tells Kurtz's intended and in the hedged explanation he gives his listeners on the *Nellie* (concerning the motivation of his visit to Kurtz's fiancée), Marlow's language is, like Kurtz's, a "pulsating stream of light, or the deceitful flow from the heart of an impenetrable darkness" (HD, p. 48).

Structure in
The Heart of Darkness

Language pulsates. Its motion, similar to the human experience of the animation of all phenomena, constitutes its illusory power, *Vorstellung*. In *Heart of Darkness*, as we shall note in *Lord Jim*, language is, paradoxically, simultaneously the revealing and deceiving animation of ideas of a conscious mind. As exemplified by Jim and by Kurtz, who is "little more than a voice," language epitomizes both the isolation of each human self ("we live, as we dream—alone" [HD, p. 28]) and the unique bond between their isolated selves. Time and again Marlow, a disengaged compassionate voice, indicates that Kurtz was unique, yet also paradigmatic. And Marlow's art of story-telling, like Kurtz's music, painting, and poetry,[75] emphasizes at once the phenomenal particular and some ultra-abstraction —engagement and detachment.

The art of Marlow's narrative does not identify the ultimate reality, for that reality is beyond human ken and is humanly experienced as an absence or hollowness. Marlow's narrative does not celebrate the phenomenal realm of human existence, for that realm is intrinsically illusory and, given human consciousness, a source of irremediable misery. It does, however, evince beauty, an aesthetic delight in using the deceptive phenomena of language to hint at the duplicity of all natural, social, and ideational phenomena. Marlow uses language, the animation of ideas of a conscious mind, to make the conscious mind of his hearer confront itself as ideationally processive. This effect accords with Schopenhauer's description of the genuine achievement of art: ideally to make the perceiving mind less aware of itself as an individual entity, be still, and (without pleasure or pain), Buddha-like, contemplate the what of the world. In this state of absorption, induced by the hearer/reader's *perception* of design in art (corresponding to humanity's *perception* of patterns in creation), the mind temporarily transcends its limitation of self; glimpses the absolute (if unknowable and possibly absent) significance beyond any imputed design in natural, social, and artistic phenomena; and ideally feels a profound compassion for every fellow human.

Marlow's narrative recalls the manner of the narrator of Hardy's *Jude the Obscure:* a compassionate employment of a mode of language transcending systematic thought and conveying impressions or "a series of seemings." In *Heart of Darkness* Marlow's use of this manner is remarked by the narrator: "to him the meaning of an episode was not inside like a kernel but outside, enveloping the tale which brought it out only as a glow brings out a haze, in the likeness of one of those misty halos that sometimes are made visible by the spectral illumination of moonshine" (HD, p. 5).[76] Like the narrator of *Jude*, the narrator of *Heart* hints at a design even while he denies its presence. He appeals to the human demand for pattern in art, in which, as in life, the *actual* phenomenon of perceived design disguises a still more pervasive *real* principle of animation evincing no system of order conceivable to human intelligence. Like Kurtz and like all human experience, Marlow's account is "hollow at the core" (HD, p. 59). Similar to the phenomenal glittering comprising its substance, Marlow's hollow narrative is a misty halo; but it is also hallowed/haloed insofar as its artistry conveys an aesthetic sense of something transcendently Other, although this Other might be nothing. Marlow's art of language, particularly well exemplified in his remark about curiosity and in his "lie" to Kurtz's fiancée, pulsates illusively into phenomenal existence and at the same time, through ironic reversals defying systematic rationality, evaporates mistlike before our mental scrutiny. It is, in short, all show, *Vorstellung*.

Just as human experience of the "show" of phenomenal existence conveys an impression of life as "gloomy circle[s] of some inferno," the reader's encounter with Conrad's phenomenal text elicits an *impression* of halo-like layering about a hollow center. Whatever makes up the plot-structure of *Heart of Darkness* fades before this impression of an emergent narrative-structure of layers. This impression of design (like the one in *Jude* and in *Lord Jim*) exists primarily in the "motion" (the perception) of the reader's search for, demand for, and positing of order in the text, as in life. Marlow's imaging of experienced facts as "ripple[s] on an unfathomable enigma" (HD, p. 43) is most apt. This image corresponds to that of the circles of hell and of the misty halos of layered narrative. The center of *Heart*, recalling the core of such fiction as "The Turn of the Screw" (discussed in Chapter 1) by Henry James, one of Conrad's mentors,[77] eludes the reader. Like *Lord Jim*, *Heart* is hollow or empty of any anticipated clear social message, even of precise identification of what "the horror" consists. Character is displaced by structure, or the intimation of structure, as the promise of a revelation of the core of Kurtz's mind is evaded in the same way as the promise of a revelation of the core of Jim's mind is evaded in *Lord Jim*. *Heart* remains a text of "folds of eloquence" (HD, p. 69)— expanding narrative layers reflective of the human experience of the phenomenal realm—around an inscrutable center. For Kurtz's story is encircled by Marlow's narrative, which is encircled by the narrator's account.[78] Although this circular pattern is not exactly the same as the architectonic spiral informing *Jude the Obscure*, it forms an expansive spiral of sorts that certainly implicates the reader in a manner identical to that of the narrative-structure of Hardy's novel.

Kurtz's frustrated quest for the meaning of what he, like Melville's Ahab,[79] construes to be the inscrutable enigma of existence becomes Marlow's pursuit of the significance of Kurtz's voice. Marlow's pursuit in turn becomes the narrator's search for the kernel-like meaning of Marlow's narrative. The narrator's search in turn becomes the reader's probing of the narrator's account. These levels of the narrative-structure are like a series of layers "in motion" radiating out from some incomprehensible, apparently void center. Reminiscent of the design of *Jude the Obscure*, the narrative pattern of *Heart of Darkness* includes the reader within the Schopenhauerian world of the story. The incomplete narrative-structure of Conrad's novella in effect remains for the reader frustratingly emergent or potential —"ripple[s] on an unfathomable enigma."

Structurally implicated in the text in this way, the reader

is denied any still-point or kernel of meaning. As in Hardy's *Jude the Obscure* and Wells's *Sea Lady*, the reader is abandoned without guidance (concerning numerous ambiguities raised in the story) at the outermost periphery of the narrative layers, a position equivalent to the outermost reaches of Kurtz's and Marlow's journey into the Congo. To Marlow "the edge of [the] colossal jungle . . . ran straight, like a ruled line, far, far away along a blue sea whose glitter was blurred by a creeping mist" (HD, p. 13). Marlow's image suggests a hypothetical fringe of glittering phenomena where, as we previously noted, the animation constituting *Vorstellung* seems to slow and where one is, at the margin of perception, on the verge of glimpsing the absolute. At the very fringe of civilization in the Congo jungle —symbolizing a hypothetical verge of the phenomenal realm —Kurtz "stepped over the edge" and Marlow "peeped over the edge" (HD, 72). They have glimpsed the Other disguised by phenomenal motion in life and language, the reality of the "stillness of an implacable force brooding with an inscrutable intention." Like Captain Ahab, Kurtz looks directly and goes mad, whereas Marlow looks aslant from the edge and so maintains his "precarious grip on existence" (HD, p. 41). Marlow "peeps" over the edge, and his story brings the narrator, and in turn the narrator brings the reader (at the periphery of the narrative), to the verge of insight into the dark hollow center at the heart of existence (including each self) and of the story.

Here we have another paradox: the reader must be at the edge in order to get a glimpse of the center; yet being at the fringe distances the reader from the center. This curious engagement and disengagement is, according to Schopenhauer, a problem inherent to the encounter with phenomena by conscious beings; and it has as its correlative in the text itself the fact that Kurtz's departure from the *center* of civilization to penetrate the *outermost* circles of existence results in the metamorphosis of his colonial, *outer* frontier encounters into the *innermost* layer of Conrad's novella. Like the paradox of the simultaneously centripetal and centrifugal spiral of Hardy's *Jude the Obscure*, Conrad's mirror-work with the notions of *inner* and *outer* exemplifies once more how the language of *Heart of Darkness* defies systematic, reductive reasoning. Equally paradoxical is the fact that language, the unique bond of humanity (Kurtz > Marlow > the narrator > the reader), consists of distancing layers; language at once relates and separates every speaker and hearer, especially separates Kurtz from the reader.

Made to relate to the narrator, Marlow, and Kurtz, and by means of the same language made to become more remote from them, respectively, the reader experiences engagement and detachment. The reader may share Marlow's sympathy for Kurtz and the narrator's interest in Marlow, but the reader is more detached than is the narrator, who is more detached than is Marlow (during his encounters), because of an increasing remoteness from the central events of the narrative. In *Heart* the emphatic "we" and the disengaged "I" make up the matrix of human consciousness (the edge of perception), and this very situation provides the context for the Schopenhauerian mode of compassion elicited by the narrative-structure of Conrad's novella. The "motion" or flow or "pulsation" of the layers of the narrative-structure of *Heart* invites the reader's curiosity, the animation of the reader's pursuit of meaning and positing of pattern. But the distancing halo-effect of these layers, around a core never revealed in characters steadily displaced by a seemingly emergent narrative-structure, also inevitably insures the reader's remoteness; the greater this sort of distance, given a bond of sympathy, the greater the potentiality for compassion of the passive, contemplative Schopenhauerian kind, rather than of the active Christian-humanist sort initially characterizing Marlow's efforts. The meaning of *Heart* lies, as the narrator observed of Marlow's manner of story-telling, "outside"—in the reader, who in a sense is "enveloping the tale"; as Marlow tells his listeners, "You fellows see more than I could" (HD, p. 28). To see more, by means of the Buddha-like compassion of the Schopenhauerian saint, peculiarly requires greater distance. Proximity to the center (involvement) requires remoteness at the edge (disengagement).

As in Hardy's novel, the combination of these extremes in Conrad's novella is achieved not systematically in terms of any philosophy but aesthetically, as *impressions* (to use Hardy's word) within the reader. Both these works privilege structure over characterization, and the narrative-structure of both at once intimates and evades a clear sense of rational design for the purpose of conveying an ethical perspective. In both these books narrative-structure implicates the reader in this ethical message by inducing in the ideal reader a "misty" consciousness (at the periphery of life and of the narrative) subtly metamorphosed into an aesthetic experience of Schopenhauerian compassion: a profoundly sympathetic, non-self-pitying, disinterested awareness of the futility of all volition in the phenomenal realm, which is determined by an impersonal force (aimless Will). The farcical glaring or glittering animation of this phenomenal realm might disguise a "heart of darkness" (nothing, void) at the core of existence, which in any event remains a place of implacable misery for necessarily "obscure" conscious beings.

In this context *Jude the Obscure* and *Heart of Darkness* are comparable, and remarkable, examples not only of Schopenhauerian aesthetics but also of the central theses of this study: (1) that in-depth characterization and fictional structure vie for dominance throughout the history of the novel; (2) that authorial intent to convey an ethical point of view (e.g., Christian-humanist or Schopenhauerian compassion) tends to result in the privileging of fictional structure, particularly narrative-structure, over (usually typical) characterization; (3) that many of the turn-of-the-century English novelists rejected by Woolf preferred structure over characterization as the primary focus of their creative energy; (4) that this predilection for structure by these novelists was as legitimate as were other attempts to simplify the dialogic tensions within the novel as a genre, particularly the similar decision (by Woolf and writers with similar convictions) to privilege characterization over structure; (5) that, given that the novel as a form eludes a restrictive poetics, the achievement of turn-of-the-century novelists who emphasized fictional structure is artistically significant and satisfying; and (6) that the achievement of these turn-of-the-century novelists is reflected in the survival of their example in the practice of certain modes of twentieth-century novels in which the management of fictional structure is a pivotal interest.

CHAPTER FIVE

.   .

.

Structure and Ethics
in Contemporary Fiction

In this chapter we move briefly to the contemporary period, the time, some have said, of the exhaustion of the novel. A consideration of two novels by Vladimir Nabokov suggests that the turn-of-the-century novelists' interest in the management of fictional structure for the purpose of ethical signification survives in some twentieth-century fiction, sometimes even when that fiction seems at first to be an unlikely inheritor of this tradition. Nabokov has often alluded to his fascination with turn-of-the-century English novelists, and his self-reflexive, playful narratives indicate the persistent *latent* connection between fictional structure and ethical concerns in fiction seemingly resistant to such a correlation.

After this latent connection has been identified in the representative contemporary example of Nabokov's work, our attention will turn to Joseph Conrad's *Lord Jim*. This novel can be read as a point of juncture: it not only once more demonstrates the correlation between fictional structure and ethics, it also anticipates the contemporary reduction (typified in Nabokov's work) of this correlation to latency.

Nabokovian Latency

In contemporary novels "inheriting" the turn-of-the-century relish for structure and "reacting" to the "Modernist" focus on character, ethical concerns may be central, peripheral, or absent. Works representative of what John Barth calls the literature of exhaustion and of the *nouveau roman* can be usefully approached in light of this turn-of-the-century tradition. Although these works include a number of significant non-turn-of-the-century influences and manifest important differences from their predecessors, they nonetheless certainly also reflect the example of turn-of-the-century English novels, an observation reinforced by Jorge Luis Borges's and Vladimir Nabokov's explicit acknowledgment of the effects on their own work of Stevenson, Wells, and Chesterton.[1]

From one point of view, the fiction of Borges, Nabokov, and Alain Robbe-Grillet—to select three representative examples —can appear to be little more than a confidence game implemented by style and expressed through structure. Typical are the unending mirrorlike reflections in Borges's "Tiön, Uqbar, Orbis Tertius," the two lines converging upon an abyss in Robbe-Grillet's *Voyeur* (1955), and the complex chess maneuvers in Nabokov's *Defense* (1930, 1964). In these and similar works characters are rendered as types,[2] as pieces in a game or creatures motivated by some obsession; plot is transformed into flawed mirror reflections or is reduced to stock patterns, to movements in a game, or to a mystery-story formula. In his prefatory remarks to *The Defense*, for example, Nabokov refers to "the moves of its [the novel's] plot" and "the semblance of a game of skill," and he particularly remarks that "the chess effects" converge "in the basic structure of the book."[3] In novels representative of the literature of exhaustion or the *nouveau roman* structure predominates. This structure can, however, remain obscure to or frustratingly unresolved for the reader, and it does not necessarily suggest an ethical dimension. This fact prevents the formulation of any steadfast rule about the correspondence between fictional structure and ethical concerns throughout the history of the novel. An author's interest in structure does not necessarily mean an interest in ethics as well, although at the turn of the nineteenth century it certainly did for many English novelists, and although even today the correspondence frequently appears in contemporary fiction.

In fact, the structural geometrical designs, jigsaw puzzles, games, and mirror-work of such books as Nabokov's *Lolita* (1955) and Robbe-Grillet's *Jealousy* (1957) and *In the Labyrinth* (1959) lure the reader into the pursuit of some meaning. This enticement becomes an end in itself in these works, a mode of entrapment in which the reader is teased into expecting some terminal explanation, an expectation deliberately frustrated by the author. The reader's pursuit of meaning in such enigmatic texts reflects the human search for meaning in the world outside the text. Although the quest emanates from within the reader and seems enticed from without, this pursuit merely amounts to activity similar to a dog's trying to catch its own tail. This is certainly the situation of the narrator of Nabokov's *Despair* (1936, 1966), who struggles to integrate his conscious sense of himself as actively self-created and his memory of himself as a creature passive before experience; in all his efforts he unwittingly discloses an unresolved paradoxical condition implying that the narrator is the creator of himself beyond his own control.

Speaking of three chapters in *The Defense* Nabokov indicates that they should remind the reader "of a certain type of chess problem where the point is not merely the finding of a mate in so many moves, but what is termed 'retrograde analysis,' the solver being required to prove from a back-cast study of the diagram position that Black's last move *could not* have been castling or *must* have been the capture of a white Pawn *en passant*" (D, p. 10). This comment alerts us to, among other matters, Nabokov's fascination with memory, but it also hints at the presence of a pattern promising closure of some sort. In *The Defense* the game of chess is likened to art, and indeed the novel is as intricately patterned as a chess game. The structure of the novel conforms to the board of fixed squares in terms of which the piecelike players engage in limited moves which somehow, as in life and in the game of chess, also convey an impression of "infinite possibilities" (D, p. 43). That impression prevents the achievement of any sense of closure finally, and the reader of *The Defense* who is enticed by the author's prefatory intimations and by the structure of the novel finds him- or herself engaged in a melancholy open-ended search for meaning or significance (sign-value). The reader is not permitted to approach the text as if it were a jigsaw puzzle, the game so attractive to youthful Luzhin, the protagonist of *The Defense*; for, as in life for Luzhin, in the text for the reader there exist no "precise combinations . . . that formed at the last moment an intelligible picture," only "curiously shaped blank spots" (D, pp. 38, 177).

Often this pursuit of intelligible meaning or the detection of sign-value is conducted in terms of reader expectations derived from previous experience with fiction. Nabokov relishes contriving tricks within old formulae. In *Despair* he has a mad Poe-esque narrator berate Arthur Conan Doyle for missing an opportunity for a last Sherlock Holmes episode in which "the very chronicler of the crime stories, Dr. Watson," should be the murderer—"a staggering surprise for the reader"; in turn, Nabokov creates in *Despair* a mystery novel in which "the murderer's identity [is] known, and . . . that of the victim [is] not."[4] By similarly alluding to the work of Jules Verne and of Doyle in *The Defense*, Nabokov warns the reader to anticipate the frustration of expectations based on previous pertinent literary models: "Only much later did [Luzhin] clarify in his own mind what it was that had thrilled him so about these two books; it was that exact and relentless unfolding pattern; Phineas [Fogg], the dummy in the top hat, wending his complex elegant way with its justifiable sacrifices . . . and Sherlock [Holmes] endowing logic with the glamour of a daydream, Sherlock composing a monograph on the ash of all known types of cigars and with this ash as with a talisman progressing through a crystal labyrinth of possible deductions to the one radiant conclusion" (D, p. 34; cf. pp. 166, 201). In *The Defense*, as in *Despair* and the fiction of Borges and Robbe-Grillet, "one radiant conclusion" fails to materialize for the reader, whose expectations of such closure with the text being read have been aroused only to be frustrated; and the pursuit of meaning is merely "infinitely" reflected in the mirror-work of, or circles back to, the novel being read. Like Luzhin and in contrast to Sherlock Holmes, the reader of *The Defense* confronts "the impossibility of inventing a rational defense, for his opponent's [i.e., the author's] aim was still hidden" (D, p. 228).

Or, more simply, that aim might be absent, as Nabokov claims (whatever the truth might be) in his introductory remarks to the revised version of *Despair*: "*Despair*, in kinship with the rest of my books, has no social comment to make, no message to bring in its teeth. It does not uplift the spiritual organ of man, nor does it show humanity the right exit" (Dr, p. 8). As the introduction to *Bend Sinister* (1947) also indicates, among other similar instances, Nabokov has often asserted that his work provides no social commentary. How, we wonder, ought the reader to correlate this disavowal with the explicit observations about Communism and Russia that surface intermittently in his novels, including *Despair*? Even if these remarks provide ironic evidence of the futility of all human effort, they are grounded in communal and social concerns. Moreover, revealing the frustration of the human search for meaning and perfection constitutes a message to the reader, who in discovering it in these texts engages in an authorially directed "retrograde analysis" (thought) and thereby exists in community with the author. Consider the implications of *Despair* when, confuting Nabokov's assertions, the narrator discloses his aim "to teach the reader a lesson" (Dr, p. 40)—both a promise and a threat—and addresses the reader directly: "Gentle reader, look at yourself in the mirror, as you seem to like mirrors so much" (Dr, p. 34). This mad, egocentric narrator is untrustworthy, a man divided against himself and in quest of himself. He confesses to uncertainty concerning his "leading motive," if any exists (Dr, p. 187), as he seeks in vain for the "extraordinary, madly happy, all-solving moment . . . of an artist's triumph" (Dr, p. 193). But his earlier remark directing the reader to look into a mirror suggests that reading novels is essentially a narcissistic activity, that the narrator is the reader's double, that the text of the novel and the text of the reader's self coalesce, one the mirror reflection of the other. The experience of this "condition" is generated by the reader's increasingly paranoiac reaction to the narrating and the (more remote) authorial opponents of *Despair*. This same experience instructs the reader about him- or herself, reflected in the text. The reader is instructed about how, in encounters with texts and the self, he or she "surpass[es] the compromising lines . . . and, moreover, fashion[s] certain bits to [his or her] liking" (Dr, p. 9).

In these texts, as in the self's encounter with life, the reader learns that reality is "other," or at least it is different from the arbitrary values humanity posits out of some ache for meaning: "it is like a nightmare when a thing gets lost, and not only can it not be discovered but there are none of those natural laws which would lend the search a certain logic, instead of which everything is absurdly shapeless and arbitrary" (Dr, p. 196). Or as Cincinnatus discovers in Nabokov's spirally structured *Invitation to a Beheading* (1938), "the bends in the corridor had not been leading him away anywhere but rather formed a great polyhedron," a prison "world which seems not a bad example of amateur craftsmanship, but is in reality calamity, horror, madness, error."[5] Such a "message," reflected in the mirror-work of text and human self, is para-ethical, to be sure; it is a statement about the imperfect artistic/natural aesthetic creation as an end in itself. Yet, significantly, this human experience of fright or frustration occurs in the context of the desire for meaning; and it is literary structure in Nabokov's works that primarily conveys the overview concerning this search, even if that overview opens to a void in which all human values appear to be essentially meaningless.

To make this observation is not to endorse the notion that fiction ought necessarily to relieve anxiety and contribute to the amelioration of human behavior;[6] and it is not to support an argument that the reader's exposure to such a void actually constitutes an invitation to desire still higher ethical standards. It does, however, imply that humanistic values can be reinforced or revised through art.[7] It also, and more pertinently to our interests in this chapter, implies that by presenting mystery-inducing structures to alert the reader to his or her tragic, pathetic, or merely absurd role as an "author" in quest of a meaningful plot and confronted with (or affronted by) the blank text of his or her own self, contemporary fiction of the *nouveau roman* or the literature of exhaustion variety evinces *latent* or vestigial ethical considerations. In this sense we can say about these works, "If we respond to them with fullness, if we seek orientation in them, then we must find them tragic and revealing documents of our age: tragic because human assertion is either subordinated or annihilated, and revealing because that is our age."[8]

The humanistic concerns inherent in these works remain latent; and in contrast to some of their turn-of-the-century predecessors, the emphasis on structure in these contemporary works hints at no therapeutic hope of a passive nostalgic or active prognostic kind. Reminiscent of Augustine's argument for the proof of God's existence, these contemporary novels point to the human yearning for meaning and perfection without endorsing the Augustinian conclusion that this longing itself implies the ontological existence of that meaning. In these writings the quest for purpose and values is left unfulfilled, thereby representing their respective authors' perception of the human condition—a condition "known" only experientially, a condition about which any intuition or rational extrapolation of guiding principles amounts to no more than a mirrorlike reflection of the unknowing, amoral self in narcissistic pursuit of itself.

Conradian Juncture

At the juncture between the turn-of-the-century correlation of fictional structure and ethical concerns typified by Stevenson's *Strange Case of Dr. Jekyll and Mr. Hyde* and the contemporary reduction of this correspondence to latency typified by Nabokov's work are certain works by Henry James and Joseph Conrad. So alert are Henry James's middle novels to the moral ambiguities and paradoxical motives of human behavior that sometimes, as we saw in his "The Turn of the Screw," they seem to displace ethical considerations with aesthetic values. However, just as characterization and structure remain in perpetual dialectic in *The Portrait of a Lady* (as we noted in Chapter 1) and in *The Ambassadors* (1903), ethics and aesthetics might also engage each other in James's middle and late novels. Perhaps, as one critic has concluded, James's "greater sensitivity

to moral distinctions is indicated by a refinement of his art."[9]
Moreover, Paul Armstrong has observed, "Although nothing *beyond* experience guarantees our meanings and values, James
discovers *within* experience the basis for a purposeful existence.
James shows that the structure of experience itself provides us
with moral imperatives through the challenge and responsibili-
ties of knowing, freedom, and care."[10]

James, we might add, expressed his sense of the value of experience, as revealed in experience, through literary structure
(for example, the hourglass shape of *The Ambassadors* and the
arch in *The Portrait of a Lady*). But he expressed the epistemological pursuit and disclosure of this meaning through characterization, which absorbed most of his attention. James's emphasis on characterization was more influential than his stress
on structure—or so it appears in the work of those reactionary novelists who experimented with the "stream of consciousness" technique, a manner certainly anticipated in James's use
of Lambert Strether as the central intelligence of *The Ambassadors*. His aesthetic refinement of literary structure struck
a number of his contemporaries as too rarefied and, as E. M.
Forster's representative reaction indicates,[11] too antagonistic to
in-depth characterization.

That James's most immediate influence on so-called Modernist fiction resided in his example of in-depth characterization
does not mean that the example of his fictional architecture
went unheeded. The latter heritage also survived to influence
other writers. One of the novelists through whom this heritage
was transmitted was Joseph Conrad, who tried to adapt James's
device of the central intelligence,[12] but who finally veered *somewhat more* toward structure than toward characterization as
a result of the pressure of epistemological uncertainties more
pervasive than even those explored by James. Conrad's *Lord
Jim* (1900) exhibits an interaction between structure and ethical

considerations that revises the correlation managed by many of his turn-of-the-century peers and anticipates the later manner of the *nouveau roman* and the literature of exhaustion.

Lord Jim, as the title announces, is ostensibly about a central character. As the novel progresses, however, Jim's thoughts, behavior, and traits become more opaque rather than more clarified. His actions exemplify, for Conrad, the essential darkness at the core of the human self. The motives of this self remain incomprehensible because of a paradoxical combination (reminiscent of Nathaniel Hawthorne's and of Henry James's shared view)[13] of freedom and fate, virtue and selfishness. This view limits any attempt at in-depth characterization; and in *Lord Jim* Marlow, who probes the meaning of Jim's behavior and narrates the bulk of the story, subtly displaces inexplicable Jim as the protagonist of the novel. But Marlow's motives, reactions, thoughts, and behavior are rendered in less depth than are Jim's; the reader is left to assess them through an account of the actual narrator of the novel, an unidentified, undramatized "privileged reader" upon whom the reader of the text must rely.[14] Whereas the novel begins with an implicit promise to reveal character, it frustrates this expectation by distancing the reader from Jim through Marlow, and then from Marlow through the narrator. Finally it suggests to the reader, whose thoughts constitute the last narrative circle, the question of whether anyone can know another person, or even oneself.

This pattern of triple layers of narrative—recording narrator, formulating Marlow, and nearly inarticulate Jim—constitutes the principle of order, or narrative-structure, imposed on a chaotic plot-structure replete with chronological ambiguities, syntactic obfuscation, and distorted perspectives. Eventually this narrative-structure displaces not only the conventional need for a coherent plot-structure but also the promise of in-depth characterization implied by the title of the novel. Narrative-

structure increasingly dominates in its contest with characterization in *Lord Jim* as an example of how people create patterns
of order in response to encounters with the inexplicable features
of existence, including unrecoverable motives behind human
behavior. In the novel authorial stress falls ultimately not upon
the unknowable in Jim or in anyone else, but upon the structure of Jim's, Marlow's, the narrator's, and the reader's pursuit
of meaning as well as on the communal matrix in which this
search occurs.

That the structure of *Lord Jim* is informed by the idea of community relates to the practice of some of Conrad's contemporary
turn-of-the-century novelists, particularly well represented (as
we saw in Chapter 1) by *The Strange Case of Dr. Jekyll and
Mr. Hyde*. In *Lord Jim* the reader seeks meaning in the narrator's
account, which is a search for meaning in Marlow's narrative,
which is a quest for meaning in Jim's words and actions. Presumably certain ethical issues inform this "social" chain. Yet,
instead of getting a Stevenson-like reinforcement of societal
valuation of "the order, the morality of an ethical progress" (LJ,
p. 255), the reader is exposed to a darkness at the center of every
human heart, a darkness obscuring clear ethical standards.

With a delusive self-image formed by sea-adventure novels
(of the sort Conrad's book is in part designed to exorcise) and
as naive as are the faithful pilgrims on the Patna, Jim clings
to an idea of honor. On the night of the Patna's disaster, his
non-action paradoxically combines cowardice and virtue; for
the fate constituted in his experience might have generated fear,
whereas the freedom affecting his concern for the doomed pilgrims might have generated compassion leading to his paralysis
and then his final jump: "You think me a cur for standing there,
but what would you have done? What! You can't tell—nobody
can tell. One must have time to turn around. . . . Where was the
kindness in making crazy with fright all those people I could

not save single-handed—that nothing could save?" (LJ, p. 74). Similarly, Jim's last action remains problematical. His manifest courage and fatal self-sacrifice before Doramin are also expressions of a selfish egotism certainly insensitive to Jewel's feelings. Whatever idea of compassion, honor, or ethics Jim or anyone else in the novel can muster is always gainsaid by its opposite. This dilemma derives from the paradoxical nature of the unknowable self, which seems to be incapable of a truly virtuous act.

Marlow's motivation, like Jim's, remains unclear. "One has no business really to get interested. It's a weakness of mine," he confesses (LJ, p. 75). In part he is curious, even nosy; but his understatement belies his compassion, so evident in his attempt to help Jim. This combination of selfish curiosity and communal compassion is epitomized in Marlow's refrain, that Jim "is one of us," an expression of wonder as well as of identity. And like his motivation, Marlow's communal commitment, his belief that "we exist only in so far as we hang together" (LJ, p. 170), includes an anticommunal "doubt of the sovereign power enthroned in a fixed standard of conduct" (LJ, p. 44). Marlow experiences the paradox of the human desire for community and ethics, and the simultaneously contesting demands of the self. Like freedom and fate at the thematic level of the novel, community and self seem at variance, though somehow they serve as essential complements, as mutually constitutive oppositions. Through his commitment to "foreign" or "alien" Jim, Marlow learns about himself, even as Jim learns about himself though his involvement with the Patna pilgrims and later with Jewel's people, even as (in Conrad's opinion) the imperialist learns about himself through his self-serving propagation of an alleged civilizing progress in foreign colonies.

If no one is capable of a genuinely virtuous act of Christian-humanist compassion or of an authentic expression of community, humanity nonetheless dreams of it. Humanity finds the *idea* of a virtuous, selfless act beautiful—hence the application of Christ imagery to Jim's final action. Ideas: as we saw in detail in Chapter 4, Conrad shared Schopenhauer's view of the function of ideas in the perpetuation of human misery. *Lord Jim* engages in a skeptical critique of the dangerous nature of ideas. In the novel attempts to assess, codify, or refine raw experience necessarily mislead and misinform; intimations of an order engendered by ideas are chimerical. But the dream of an order resolving the paradoxical dilemmas of an existential condition, made up of a sealike swirl of fragmentary experiences, can be aesthetically satisfying (as Oscar Wilde also believed [Chapter 1]). Consider Marlow's reference to the example of Stein, who extrapolates an idea of order from *his* perception of beauty in the butterfly:

I respected the intense, almost passionate, absorption with which he looked at the butterfly, as though on the bronze sheen of these frail wings, in the white tracings, in the gorgeous markings, he could see other things, an image of something as perishable and defying destruction as these delicate and lifeless tissues displaying a splendour unmarred by death.

"Marvelous!" he repeated, looking up at me. "Look! The beauty—but that is nothing—look at the accuracy, the harmony. And so fragile! And so strong! And so exact! This is Nature—the balance of colossal forces. Every star is so—and every blade of grass stands so—and the mighty Kosmos in perfect equilibrium produces—this. This wonder; this masterpiece of Nature—the great artist."   *(LJ, p. 158)*

Out of "the destructive element" that is life, Stein has seized upon the butterfly as an emblem of beauty, and this attraction to attributed beauty has led him to dream of an idea of cosmic order. Stein seems deliberately to ignore the destructive caterpillar stage of the butterfly; still, the butterfly is also really present.

So too with the human self, at once ignoble and lordly, as exemplified by Jim: the caterpillar mode of the self is egotistical and selfish, whereas the butterfly mode of the self is communal and sacrificial. The former, the heart of darkness, corresponds to silence, the latter to language. Language is a two-edged implement which at once conceals and reveals. Language, for Conrad, conveys ideas and so, given the dangerous nature of ideas, it deludes, while it seems to enlighten, speaker and hearer alike. The "weird power in a spoken word" (LJ, p. 134) especially illuminates *and* obscures the idea of community. That without language community apparently fails is suggested by Marlow's exposure to an "utter solitude" in which "human speech itself, seemed to have passed away out of existence, living for a while longer in [his] memory, as though [he] had been the last of mankind" (LJ, p. 243). Moreover, the multi-narrative layers of *Lord Jim* suggest that language functions as the adhesive of community.

Silence also reveals truth, the truth of the individual self, so alone that to a significant degree it always remains outside the help of communal identity. This is one meaning of Jim's difficulty with language and his dying gesture of placing his hand over his lips. Silence frames language, even as the dark cosmos frames the colorful butterfly. Silence defines the origin of language, even as ideas, the substance of language, seem to emerge from nowhere. But just as the symmetrical beauty of the butterfly elicits the dream of an aesthetic order behind phenomenal existence (i.e., if the comparatively "ugly" caterpillar stage is ignored), the wonder of language encourages humanity to dream of ideal communal values (i.e., if language's destructive capacity or its inadequacy in conveying "innumerable shades" [LJ, p. 76] are overlooked). It is principally in accordance with this ideal that we can say, as two critics have observed, that for Conrad and Marlow language is a "realm of circumscribed intelligibility rescuing one from darkness" and "give[s] the world that order that makes it tolerable."[15] In Lord Jim language and its idea/ideal of community is a destructive element which also keeps humanity afloat.

Lord Jim intimates that it will yield some truth about a character. Steadily, however, it displaces this hint with an emerging emphasis on a three-tiered narrative-structure. In turn this structure seems to correspond to ethical and communal issues raised in the novel, though in fact those concerns remain vexed and unresolved.

This tension between characterization and structure, and between self and society, freedom and fate, recalls a very similar dialogism in Emily Brontë's Wuthering Heights. Although Brontë's novel shares with Lord Jim the same irresolution of these tensions, her book finally tends to privilege characterization somewhat over structure. As we saw in Chapter 1, Brontë manages narrative-structure in her novel to alert the reader to how ideas of social order are often too narrow or inaccurate, given the enigma of an inclusive polymorphous human community. She suggests that even though the reading of the text of society necessarily remains inconclusive in structural terms, yet that social text is nonetheless valued from her point of view as something very real. She emphasizes character as the mysterious cipher of that enigmatic social text.

In contrast, the irresolution of tensions in the narrative-structure of Conrad's Lord Jim raises more vexing questions not only about the authenticity of compassion and community, but also about the reality and value of society itself. Conrad suggests that the idea of community might be as much a fabrication as is a fictional text, such as any sea-adventure book read by Jim. Whereas Brontë leaves the reader of her narrative to dwell upon character in light of the inexplicable and non-unitary nature of concrete community, Conrad leaves the reader of his story to ponder structure in light of the human dream of design elicited not only by the unfathomableness of human motives, but even more so by the inexplicable nature of an apparently structureless creation. Representing a response to this sense of absence in the cosmos, the aesthetic structure of *Lord Jim* is like Stein's butterfly.

Nevertheless, just as Brontë's structure-distorting polarization toward characterization highlights unresolved dialogic communal questions, Conrad's self-reflexive polarization toward structure highlights the unresolved ontological questions behind the ethical issues encountered by the reader of *Lord Jim*. In this regard, a passage spoken by Marlow about Jim's life seems to describe Conrad's technique in this novel. Here Conrad seems to warn the reader away from any further pursuit of the convergence of ethical truth and aesthetic structure: "I saw it vividly, as though in our progress through the lofty silent rooms amongst fleeting gleams of light and the sudden revelations of human figures stealing with flickering flames within unfathomable and pellucid depths, we had approached nearer the absolute Truth, which like Beauty itself, floats elusive, obscure, half-submerged, in the silent still waters of mystery" (LJ, p. 165). Conrad's novel manifests stylistic pellucid depths punctuated by flickering illumination, or insights, and a "half-submerged" structure seeming to reveal some ethical truth. This structure, in fact, might just as well become the means by which the unwary reader is wrecked, like the Patna, and drowns, like the idea-laden pilgrims dreaming of an elusive ideal.

In *Lord Jim* ethical questions surface only to be evaded. Answers to these questions are as elusive as are the attempts at in-depth characterization of Jim and the disclosure of ontological truth in the novel. In *Lord Jim* structure and style become ends in themselves well beyond the example of Henry James. They are certainly not completely divorced from the ethical considerations raised in the novel, but they are unable to provide the reader with the sort of directiveness evident in Stevenson's, Kipling's, Wells's, and Bennett's stress on human potentialities, or in Brontë's stress on a real polymorphous community, or in James's stress on moral imperatives. Like Stein's butterfly, the symmetrical beauty of the narrative-structure of *Lord Jim* suggests some larger order, purpose, truth; yet, just as Stein's extrapolation of the idea of order from the butterfly is arbitrary in its emphasis on one feature of nature, so too whatever ideas of *finished* order or *resolved* message the reader might perceive in the structure of this novel derive from the reader, whose thoughts comprise the outermost layer of the novel's narrative.

In *Lord Jim* Conrad, it appears, deliberately frustrates reader expectations concerning the relation between fictional structure and ethical concerns so prominent in the novels of his immediate predecessors and his peers. He does so, in contrast to Brontë's example, to create a para-ethical artistry. In effect, Conrad's practice anticipates (though hardly determines) the fascination with structure characteristic of the *nouveau roman* and the literature of exhaustion. Like the fiction in these two later modes, *Lord Jim* exhibits a structure beautiful in itself, at once nostalgically evoking the human desire for a standard of values in life and "realistically" frustrating that desire in the reader. In this way the reader's epistemological search is reduced to a matter of relativity equivalent to the proverbial attribution of beauty to the eye of the beholder. If the language constituting the style and structure of *Lord Jim* appears beautiful, its beauty, like that of Stein's butterfly, emerges from the destructive element which is the empirical self, confronted by experiences, refusing to signify beyond the arbitrary values assigned to them by that self. In the absence of Stein's Nature,

in the absence of the author (Conrad) from his novel, this perceiving reader-self becomes—whether it will or not, hence its
fate and its coerced freedom—its own artist creating its own
meaning in the text of its own self.[16]

Conrad's management of the correlation of fictional structure and ethical considerations indicates that the in-structing,
paradoxical self, however much it longs for a standard of ethics
(a clear vision of its options), might or might not evince some
ultimate informing meaning. After Conrad, writers like Borges,
Nabokov, and Robbe-Grillet reduce to latency, at best, the relation between fictional structure and ethics. They focus on
fictional structure as an end in itself so as to represent the
essentially solipsistic activity of the self undergoing experiences characterized by unfathomable principles or by the absence of any principles. Although the fascination with structure
so prominent in their fiction operates outside any manifest
questions about ethical considerations, the issue of reduction
or latency remains. Insofar as the sleuthing reader puzzles over
the structural parts of such self-contained texts, is frustrated
in his or her expectations, and perhaps is made aware of the
distortion or absence of standards of value in the text, he or
she experiences a vestige of the older correspondence between
fictional structure and ethics.

Emphatic structural management, which tends toward
determined characterization, generally is not today critically
regarded as an artistic achievement equivalent to complex
in-depth characterization in a novel. We tend to endorse Virginia Woolf's belief, as we saw in Chapter 1, that the novel
evolved primarily to express character. Woolf's position is a
simplification of the problem abiding between characterization
and structure in the fiction of her Victorian predecessors, in
Brontë's *Wuthering Heights,* for example. In fact, throughout
the history of the novel characterization and structure appar-

Fictional Structure and Ethics

ently have evinced a dialectical interaction suggesting their aesthetic equality; and some authors have, in practice and statement, not shared the position articulated by Woolf and other novelists with similar convictions. Many turn-of-the-century English writers similarly simplified this particular feature of the dialogic nature of fiction by stressing structure, a preference still active in certain modes of fiction practiced toward the end of the twentieth century. This emphasis on structure by turn-of-the-century English novelists and their successors accords with their interest in ethical concerns, whether these concerns be manifest (an author's didactic or manipulative intent) or vestigial (a reader's conditioned expectation); for within the characterization-structure dialectic intrinsic to the novel, a positive correspondence often exists between authorial stress on fictional structure and authorial and/or reader interest in the ethos (options) of the human community.

Notes

Introduction

1. Linda Dowling, *Language and Decadence in the Victorian Fin de Siècle* (Princeton: Princeton University Press, 1986).
2. Wayne C. Booth, *The Company We Keep: An Ethics of Fiction* (Berkeley: University of California Press, 1988). On the nature of some constraints on explicitly ethical approaches to literature, see Tobin Siebers, *The Ethics of Criticism* (Ithaca: Cornell University Press, 1988).
3. Wolfgang Iser, *The Implied Reader: Patterns of Communication in Prose Fiction from Bunyan to Beckett* (Baltimore: The Johns Hopkins University Press, 1974), pp. 285, 293.
4. Peter Brooks, *Reading for the Plot: Design and Intention in Narrative* (New York: Knopf, 1984).
5. J. Hillis Miller, "Is There an Ethics of Reading?" *Reading Narrative: Form, Ethics, and Ideology*, ed. James Phelan (Columbus: Ohio State University Press, 1989), p. 86.
6. *Lives of the Eminent Philosophers* (New York: Harcourt, 1925), book 10, chapter 30.
7. Jerome J. McGann, *Social Values and Poetic Acts: The Historical Judgment of Literary Work* (Cambridge: Harvard University Press, 1988).
8. Interestingly, Daniel R. Schwarz has concluded that, despite differences separating various strands of Anglo-American literary criticism, a common concern in it has been how form discovers the meaning of content (*The Humanistic Heritage: Critical Theories of the English Novel from James to Hillis Miller* [Philadelphia: University of Pennsylvania Press, 1986], p. 4).

1. Fictional Structure and Ethics

1. Jefferson Hunter, *Edwardian Fiction* (Cambridge: Harvard University Press, 1982); Jonathan Rose, *The Edwardian Temperament: 1895–1919* (Athens: Ohio University Press, 1986).

2. John Batchelor, *The Edwardian Novelists* (London: Duckworth, 1982).

3. *The Autobiography of G. K. Chesterton* (New York: Sheed and Ward, 1936), pp. 87–90, 142, 286.

4. Gilbert K. Chesterton, *Orthodoxy* (New York: Lane, 1908), pp. 77, 130; *Manalive* (London: Nelson, 1912), pp. 209, 224; *Come to Think of It* (London: Macmillan, 1932), p. 127.

5. J. Hillis Miller, *The Ethics of Reading: Kant, de Man, Eliot, Trollope, James, and Benjamin* (New York: Columbia University Press, 1987), p. 2. An important statement on how narrative literature calls for a human response is made by Wayne C. Booth, *The Company We Keep: An Ethics of Fiction* (Berkeley: University of California Press, 1988).

6. See John Allen Quintus, "The Moral Implications of Oscar Wilde's Aestheticism," *Texas Studies in Literature and Language* 22 (1980): 559–74; Richard Ellmann, *Oscar Wilde* (New York: Knopf, 1988), pp. 300–59.

7. Several arguments in this and the last chapter appeared in different, much shortened form in "Fictional Structure and Ethics in the Edwardian, Modern and Contemporary Novel," *Philological Quarterly* 62 (1984): 287–311.

8. Robert Louis Stevenson, *The Strange Case of Dr. Jekyll and Mr. Hyde*, ed. Jenni Calder (Harmondsworth, England: Penguin, 1979), pp. 58, 86, 63, 29.

9. Oscar Wilde, *The Picture of Dorian Gray* (Harmondsworth, England: Penguin, 1949), pp. 5–6.

10. Wilde, *The Picture of Dorian Gray*, pp. 68, 241.

11. John Allen Quintus, "The Moral Implications of Oscar Wilde's Aestheticism," *Texas Studies in Literature and Language* 22 (1980): 559–74.

12. Wilde, *The Picture of Dorian Gray*, pp. 221, 158.

13. Angus Fletcher, *Allegory: The Theory of a Symbolic Mode* (Ithaca: Cornell University Press, 1964), p. 180.

14. Fletcher, *Allegory*, pp. 360–61.
15. See William Bellamy, *The Novels of Wells, Bennett and Galsworthy, 1880–1910* (London: Routledge and Kegan Paul, 1971).
16. This character/structure dichotomy seems to correspond to the deconstructionist distinction between symbol and allegory, the latter expressing "the unveiling of an authentically temporal destiny" and the former expressing the engagement of time as "merely a matter of contingency." Paul de Man, "The Rhetoric of Temporality," in *Interpretation: Theory and Practice,* ed. Charles S. Singleton (Baltimore: The Johns Hopkins University Press, 1969), pp. 173–209.
17. Elliot L. Gilbert, *The Good Kipling: Studies in the Short Story* (Manchester, England: Manchester University Press, 1972), pp. 21–49. My comments in this section of Chapter 1 appeared in somewhat different form as "Hesitation in Kipling's 'The Phantom 'Rickshaw,'" *English Literature in Transition* 29 (1986): 48–53.
18. J. M. S. Tompkins, *The Art of Rudyard Kipling* (London: Methuen, 1959), p. 118.
19. Rudyard Kipling, *Something of Myself,* in *Kipling: A Selection of His Stories and Prose,* ed. John Beecroft (Garden City: Doubleday, 1956), p. 402; *The Phantom 'Rickshaw and Other Tales* (New York: A. L. Burt, 1900), p. iii.
20. See *Selected Prose and Poetry of Rudyard Kipling* (Garden City: Doubleday, 1937), William Lyon Phelps's edition of *Selected Stories from Kipling* (Garden City: Doubleday, 1924), and John Beecroft's *Kipling: A Selection of His Stories and Prose.*
21. "The Tales of Rudyard Kipling," *Edinburgh Review* 174 (July 1891): 132–41; Edmund Gosse, "Rudyard Kipling," *Century Magazine* 42 (1891): 906. Walter Morris Hart oddly complains that the ghost in the story talks too much and lacks dignity: *Kipling: The Story-Teller* (Berkeley: University of California Press, 1918), pp. 21–22.
22. Although Norman Page does not analyze the story, he does suggest that it is a landmark in the development of Kipling's art: *Kipling Companion* (New York: Macmillan, 1984), pp. 115–16.
23. Tzvetan Todorov, *The Fantastic: A Structural Approach to a Literary Genre,* trans. Richard Howard (Cleveland: The Press of Case Western University, 1973), p. 25.
24. Rudyard Kipling, "The Phantom 'Rickshaw," in *The Writings in*

Prose and Verse of Rudyard Kipling (New York: Scribner's Sons, 1905), 5:22, 23. Page references to subsequent quotations from this edition appear parenthetically in the text.

25. This revision is remarked by Louis L. Cornell, "The Development of Kipling's Prose from 1883 through 'Plain Tales from the Hills,'" *English Literature in Transition* 7 (1964): 197; and again in Cornell, *Kipling and India* (London: Macmillan, 1966), pp. 107–8.

26. Todorov, *The Fantastic*, p. 31. "The haunting of Pansay is suspended between the credulity of the 'I' and the scepticism of Dr. Heatherlegh" (Tompkins, *The Art of Rudyard Kipling*, p. 199).

27. Not all readers, however, have been careful to maintain the uncertain, detached response suggested by the narrator. Some have asserted that the tale reveals Kipling's belief in the spectral (for example, Bonamy Dobree, *Rudyard Kipling: Realist and Fabulist* [London: Oxford University Press, 1967], p. 27); and some have asserted that the story is about mental illness (for example, Peter Penzoldt, *The Supernatural in Fiction* [London: Peter Nevill, 1952], pp. 118–45).

28. An association between pity and the management of narrative voice in another story by Kipling is briefly mentioned in Tim Bascom's somewhat unreliable "Secret Imperialism: The Reader's Response to the Narrator in 'The Man Who Would Be King,'" *English Literature in Transition* 31 (1988): 162–73.

29. Tzvetan Todorov, *The Poetics of Prose*, trans. Richard Howard (Ithaca: Cornell University Press, 1977), pp. 179–89.

30. Tobin Siebers, "Hesitation, History, and Reading: Henry James's *The Turn of the Screw*," *Texas Studies in Literature and Language* 25 (1983): 558–73. Others who have objected to certain limitations of Todorov's theory include Eric S. Rabkin, *The Fantastic in Literature* (Princeton: Princeton University Press, 1976), p. 118; and Rosemary Jackson, *Fantasy: The Literature of Subversion* (London: Methuen, 1981), p. 91. Contrary to Siebers's position is Daniel R. Schwarz, who remarks James's assessment of the tension between aesthetics and moral, and who attributes to James a polarization toward the practice of "allowing a text to generate its own aesthetic" (*The Humanistic Heritage*, p. 22). A good survey of the controversy over this story (and an unfortunate reduction of the work to a pulp horror tale) appears in Peter G. Beidler, *Ghosts, De-*

mons, and Henry James (Columbia: University of Missouri Press, 1989).

31. Robert Scholes and Robert Kellogg, *The Nature of Narrative* (London: Oxford University Press, 1966), p. 171.

32. Walter Reed, "The Problem with a Poetics of the Novel," *Novel* 9 (1976): 101–13; Jonathan Culler, "Problems in the Theory of Fiction," *Diacritics* 14 (1984): 2–11.

33. On the tendency of Victorian novels to overflow their boundaries, see J. Hillis Miller, *The Form of Victorian Fiction: Thackeray, Dickens, Trollope, George Eliot, Meredith, and Hardy* (Notre Dame: University of Notre Dame Press, 1968); Peter Conrad, *The Victorian Treasure House* (London: Collins, 1973), p. 44; and Peter K. Garrett, *The Victorian Multiplot Novel: Studies in Dialogical Form* (New Haven: Yale University Press, 1980).

34. *Letters and Private Papers of William Makepeace Thackeray* (Cambridge: Harvard University Press, 1946), 3:67.

35. H. G. Wells, *Experiment in Autobiography* (New York: Macmillan, 1934), p. 423. On characterization and structure in this novel, see respectively Lucille Herbert, "*Tono-Bungay:* Tradition and Experiment," *Modern Language Quarterly* 33 (1972): 140–55; Kenneth B. Newell, *Structure in Four Novels by H. G. Wells* (The Hague: Mouton, 1968), pp. 75–83.

36. Passages from Woolf's notebook appear in Margaret Church, *Structure and Theme: "Don Quixote" to James Joyce* (Columbus: Ohio State University Press, 1983), p. 177.

37. Henry James, "Preface to the New York Edition," *The Portrait of a Lady*, ed. Robert D. Bamberg (New York: Norton, 1975), pp. 3–15.

38. *William Faulkner: Three Decades of Criticism*, ed. Frederick J. Hoffman and Olga W. Vickery (New York: Harcourt, Brace and World, 1963), pp. 73, 82. See especially Donald M. Kartiganer, *The Fragile Thread: The Meaning of Form in Faulkner's Novels* (Amherst: University of Massachusetts Press, 1979).

39. M. M. Bakhtin, *The Dialogic Imagination: Four Essays*, ed. Michael Holquist (Austin: University of Texas Press, 1981), pp. 262–63.

40. Arnold Bennett, *The Author's Craft* (New York: Doran, 1914), pp. 22–23.

154

Notes to Chapter 1

41. Jacob Tonson [Arnold Bennett], "H. G. Wells," *New Age*, 4 May
1909.
42. Virginia Woolf, "Mr. Bennett and Mrs. Brown," *Collected Essays*
(New York: Harcourt, Brace and World, 1967), 1:319. On the limits
of Woolf's revolt against the Edwardians, see James Gindon, *Harvest of a Quiet Eye: The Novel of Compassion* (Bloomington: Indiana University Press, 1971), pp. 203–4.
43. Rachel Blau DuPlessis, *Writing Beyond the Ending: Narrative
Strategies of Twentieth-Century Women Writers* (Bloomington:
University of Indiana Press, 1985); Susan Stanford Friedman,
"Lyric Subversion of Narrative in Women's Writing: Virginia
Woolf and the Tyranny of Plot," *Reading Narrative: Form, Ethics,
and Ideology*, ed. James Phelan (Columbus: Ohio State University
Press, 1989), pp. 162–85.
44. H. G. Wells, *Babes in the Darkling Wood* (New York: Alliance
Book Company, 1940), p. x.
45. Ellen Frank, *Literary Architecture: Essays Toward a Tradition*
(Berkeley: University of California Press, 1979), pp. 36–41, 256.
46. Joseph A. Kestner, *The Spatiality of the Novel* (Detroit: Wayne
State University Press, 1978), p. 77.
47. Joseph A. Kestner discusses the preeminence of architectural space
in fiction (*The Spatiality of the Novel*, pp. 110–33).
48. *Henry James and H. G. Wells*, ed. Leon Edel and Gordon N. Ray
(Urbana: University of Illinois Press, 1958), p. 264; Wells, *Experiment in Autobiography*, p. 415.
49. George Eliot, "The Progress of Fiction as an Art," as cited in
Robert A. Colby, *Fiction with a Purpose: Major and Minor Nineteenth-Century Novels* (Bloomington: Indiana University Press,
1967), p. 25. See also *The Writings of George Eliot* (Boston:
Houghton-Mifflin, 1908), 21:296.
50. John P. Farrell, "Reading the Text of Community in *Wuthering
Heights*," *ELH* 56 (1989): 173–208.
51. Inga-Stina Ewbank, *Their Proper Sphere: A Study of the Brontë
Sisters as Early-Victorian Female Novelists* (Cambridge: Harvard
University Press, 1966), pp. 128–41.
52. Mary Visick, *The Genius of Wuthering Heights* (Hong Kong: Hong
Kong University Press, 1958), pp. 57–60.

53. John K. Mathison, "Nelly Dean and the Power of *Wuthering Heights*," *Nineteenth-Century Fiction* 11 (1957): 298–305.

54. In "Social Morality and Individual Ideal" (in *Freedom and Resentment and Other Essays* [London: Methuen, 1974], pp. 27–29), P. F. Strawson notes that in-depth characterization can lead to a confusion of ethical perspective in the reader, but that this result is acceptable because such characterization pleases the reader's imagination. The complexities and confusions involved in detailed characterization are documented by Martin Price, *Forms of Life: Character and Moral Imagination in the Novel* (New Haven: Yale University Press, 1983).

55. On open form, see Alan Friedman, *The Turn of the Novel* (London: Oxford University Press, 1966); on ethos and pathos in characterization, see Anthony Channell Hilfer, *The Ethics of Intensity in American Fiction* (Austin: University of Texas Press, 1981). Since plot-structure is also a consideration in fiction it is pertinent to note Robert L. Caserio's conclusion that when writers lose interest in story and plot, they appear to distrust the significance and moral value of human activity: *Plot, Story and the Novel: From Dickens to the Modern Period* (Princeton: Princeton University Press, 1979).

56. James Joyce, *A Portrait of the Artist as a Young Man*, in *The Portable James Joyce* (New York: Viking, 1947), p. 525. For the point about Joyce I am indebted to Wayne C. Booth, *The Rhetoric of Fiction* (Chicago: University of Chicago Press, 1961).

57. The complete degree to which the "Modernists" interiorize whatever structure their works contain is documented by Margaret Church, *Structure and Theme: "Don Quixote" to James Joyce* (Columbus: Ohio State University Press, 1983).

58. Thomas Hardy, *Jude the Obscure* (Harmondsworth, England: Penguin, 1978), p. 39.

59. Structure in Hardy's fiction, for instance, is the chief factor in creating tragic effect: see Dale Kramer, *Thomas Hardy: The Forms of Tragedy* (Detroit: Wayne State University Press, 1975). Ian Gregor's argument, in *The Great Web: The Form of Hardy's Major Fiction* (Totowa, New Jersey: Rowman and Littlefield, 1974), that form is only provisional in Hardy's fiction is true only in a most complex sense, as we shall see in Chapter 4.

60. Virginia Woolf, *Collected Essays* (New York: Harcourt, Brace and World, 1967), 1:337.

61. The nineteenth-century interest in replacing subjectivity with a comparatively self-denying objectivity is discussed in James Helprin's *Egotism and Self Discovery in the Victorian Novel* (New York: Burt Franklin, 1974). Omniscient narration and collective consciousness are associated by Miller, *The Form of Victorian Fiction*, pp. 53–90.

62. Arnold Bennett, *Anna of the Five Towns* (Harmondsworth, England: Penguin, 1963), p. 57 (italics added).

63. I am reversing the sense of "open" and "closed" form argued by Alan Friedman, *The Turn of the Novel*. Pertinent reapplications of these two terms appear in *The Role of the Reader: Explorations in the Semiotics of Texts* (Bloomington: Indiana University Press, 1979), in which Umberto Eco argues that seemingly closed works evidence a management of language that actually maximizes interpretative indeterminacy for the unsuspecting reader; and in *Vladimir's Carrot: Modern Drama and the Modern Imagination* (Chicago: University of Chicago Press, 1987), in which John Peter extrapolates from Schopenhauer's thought a distinction between how a closed play excludes the viewer from questions about ultimate meanings and how an open play encourages the viewer to experience those questions personally. An interesting recent defense of the use of typical characterization appears in Jane Tompkins, *Sensational Designs: The Cultural Work of American Fiction, 1790–1860* (New York: Oxford University Press, 1985).

64. *The Early Writings in Science and Science Fiction by H. G. Wells*, ed. Robert Philmus and David Y. Hughes (Berkeley: University of California Press, 1975), p. 94.

65. H. G. Wells, *The Conquest of Time* (London: Watts, 1942), pp. 17, 35, 40. Cf. Wells, *Star Begotten* (London: Chatto and Windus, 1937), pp. 139, 172.

66. On dialogism of voice in this novel, see Randall Craig, *The Tragi-Comic Novel: Studies in a Fictional Mode from Meredith to Joyce* (Newark: University of Delaware Press, 1989), pp. 79–98.

67. Bennett, *Anna of the Five Towns*, p. 25.

68. Georges Poulet, *Studies in Human Time*, trans. Elliott Coleman (Baltimore: The Johns Hopkins University Press, 1956); Margaret

Church, *Time and Reality: Studies in Contemporary Fiction* (Chapel Hill: University of North Carolina Press, 1963); Shiv K. Kumar, *Bergson and the Stream of Consciousness Novel* (New York: New York University Press, 1963); W. J. Harvey, *Character in the Novel* (Ithaca: Cornell University Press, 1965); Jerome Hamilton Buckley, *The Triumph of Time: A Study of the Victorian Concepts of Time, History, Progress, and Decadence* (Cambridge: Harvard University Press, 1966); Morris Beja, *Epiphany in the Modern Novel* (Seattle: University of Washington Press, 1971); A. A. Medilow, *Time and the Novel* (New York: Humanities Press, 1972); and David Leon Higdon, *Time and English Fiction* (London: Macmillan, 1977).

69. Late in life Wells revised his approach to history as a measurement of human destiny, and, though he never dismissed history, he suspected then that it often served to reinforce the framework impeding human development. History is necessarily retrospective, Wells then concluded, whereas a vision of human destiny is prospective. Moreover, although (as *The Undying Fire* [1919] makes clear) all history converges into some unity, this cohesion—the principle of order governing the universe—remains unknowable to anyone at any given point in time except perhaps as a transient near-mystical sensation or intuition experienced by certain average individuals who become unwitting prophets of human destiny.

70. Wells, *The Conquest of Time*, pp. 42, 63.

71. H. G. Wells, *The Work, Wealth and Happiness of Mankind* (London: Heinemann, 1932), p. 69.

72. On freedom and fate in Wells's thought, see John R. Reed, *The Natural History of H. G. Wells* (Athens: Ohio University Press, 1982), pp. 137–76.

73. Philmus and Hughes, *The Early Writings*, p. 139. See also Roslynn D. Haynes's discussion of Wells's attitudes toward individuality and collectivism, personal freedom and species predestination, and typical members representing the entire species, in *H. G. Wells: Discoverer of the Future* (New York: New York University Press, 1980), pp. 118, 125, 132, 167.

74. Wells, *The Conquest of Time*, p. 42.

75. H. G. Wells, *Experiment in Autobiography* (New York: Macmillan, 1934), pp. 75, 76, 80, 104.

76. H. G. Wells, "Jude the Obscure," *Saturday Review* 81 (1896): 153–54. More commentary on Hardy's typological characterization appears in Virginia R. Hyman's *Ethical Perspective in the Novels of Thomas Hardy* (Port Washington, New York: Kennikat, 1975) and Geoffery Thurley's *The Psychology of Hardy's Novels* (Atlantic Highlands, New Jersey: Humanities Press, 1975).

77. H. G. Wells, "The Novel of Types," *Saturday Review* 81 (1896): 23–24.

78. John Galsworthy, "Twelve Books—And Why," *Saturday Review of Literature* 4 (3 December 1927): 364. See also Galsworthy, *Candelabra* (New York: Scribner's Sons, 1933).

79. Terry Eagleton, *Marxism and Literary Criticism* (Berkeley: University of California Press, 1976), p. 29. Note too an instance of the Hegelean cast of Wells's thought in spite of his explicit hostility to Hegel's ideas, the latter remarked by W. Warren Wagar, *H. G. Wells and the World State* (New Haven: Yale University Press, 1961), p. 107, note 102.

80. See *Literary Uses of Typology from the Late Middle Ages to the Present*, ed. Earl Miner (Princeton: Princeton University Press, 1977).

81. See Jerome Bump, *Gerard Manley Hopkins* (Boston: Twayne, 1982), and Herbert L. Sussman, *Fact into Figure: Typology in Carlyle, Ruskin, and the Pre-Raphaelite Brotherhood* (Columbus: Ohio University Press, 1979). Pertinent too is Richard Ellmann's observation that although the "Edwardian writers rejected Christianity . . . they felt free to *use* it, for while they did not need religion they did need religious metaphors": *Golden Codgers: Biographical Speculation* (London: Oxford University Press, 1972), p. 116.

82. Frank Kermode, *The Art of Telling: Essays on Fiction* (Cambridge: Harvard University Press, 1983), pp. 39–42.

83. "In the Abyss" has been read, simply, as expressing the theme of apotheosis also found in other works by Wells (Bernard Bergonzi, *The Early H. G. Wells* [Manchester, England: Manchester University Press, 1961], p. 73); as satirizing Christianity (Patrick Parrinder, *H. G. Wells* [Edinburgh: Oliver and Boyd, 1970], pp. 37–38); as reflecting the possible development of an evolutionary challenge to human civilization (Jack Williamson, *H. G. Wells: Critic of Progress* [Baltimore: Mirage Press, 1973], p. 67); as cre-

ating a metaphor for the urban poor (John Batchelor, *The Edwardian Novelists*, pp. 6–7); and as evidencing Wells's use of "the prospect" in his works (John Reed, *The Natural History of H. G. Wells* [Athens: Ohio University Press, 1982], p. 45). Reed, incidentally, wonders whether the short story is indebted to Henry James's study of humanity's confrontation with its own fear in "Owen Wingrave" (p. 249, n. 9). My comments in this section of Chapter 1 appeared in somewhat different form in "The In-Struction of Wells's 'In the Abyss,'" *Studies in Short Fiction* 24 (1987): 155–59.

84. Management of structure in Wells's early fiction is considered, for example, by Darko Suvin, "A Grammar of Form and a Criticism of Fact: *The Time Machine* as a Structural Model for Science Fiction," *H. G. Wells and Modern Science Fiction*, ed. Darko Suvin and Robert M. Philmus (Lewisburg, Pennsylvania: Bucknell University Press, 1977), pp. 90–115. Management of structure in Wells's later fiction is discussed by William J. Scheick, *The Splintering Frame: The Later Fiction of H. G. Wells* (Victoria, British Columbia: University of Victoria, 1984).

85. "In the Abyss," *The Short Stories of H. G. Wells* (London: Ernest Benn, 1927), p. 434. Page references to subsequent quotations from this edition appear parenthetically in the text. This edition, incidentally, differs from the first version of the story in *Pearson's Magazine* (August 1896) principally in two paragraphs which Wells added to his revision.

86. On Wells's tendency to allegorize in his early romances, see Bergonzi, *The Early H. G. Wells*, and Frank McConnell, *The Science Fiction of H. G. Wells* (New York: Oxford University Press, 1981). McConnell replies to Bergonzi by arguing that Wells's allegorical meanings are complex, an intricate integration of ambiguous, even contradictory ideas. In this regard John Huntington focuses on the dialectic between directed and undirected thought and on the coexistence of two-world oppositions in Wells's early writings: *The Logic of Fantasy: H. G. Wells and Science Fiction* (New York: Columbia University Press, 1982).

87. On the place of science in Wells's vision of the future, see (most recently) Roslynn D. Haynes, *H. G. Wells: Discoverer of the Future* (New York: New York University Press, 1980).

Notes to Chapter 2

2. Compassion and Fictional Structure

1. An earlier version of this chapter appeared as "Compassion and Fictional Structure: The Example of Gissing and Bennett," *Studies in the Novel* 15 (1983): 293–313.
2. Arnold Bennett, "George Gissing," *Academy* no. 1441 (16 December 1899): 725; *Letters of Arnold Bennett: Volume II, 1899–1915*, ed. James Hepburn (London: Oxford University Press, 1968), pp. 36–145.
3. That is, some critics have argued that Gissing was unable to achieve his goal of pure art because a moral mission inevitably emerges in his work: for example, Jacob Korg, "Division of Purpose in George Gissing," *PMLA* 70 (1955): 323–36. On the other hand, an excellent argument has been made indicating that this very tension defines Gissing's art at its best, that "Gissing's solution . . . will be to recombine . . . the privileged ideological viewpoint of the alienated intellectual and the ethical mission . . . in such a way that the fate of the first will be able to serve as a commentary on and a dramatization of the content of the second": Fredric Jameson, "Authentic *Ressentement:* The 'Experimental' Novels of Gissing," *Nineteenth-Century Fiction* 31 (1976): 127–49.
4. Adrian Poole, *Gissing in Context* (London: Macmillan, 1975), p. 64; David Grylls, *The Paradox of Gissing* (London: Allen and Unwin, 1986), p. 17; Patrick Bridgwater, *George Moore and German Pessimism* (Durham, England: University of Durham, 1988), p. 54.
5. Details of this revision and an argument for its superiority to the first version are presented in Joseph J. Wolff, "Gissing's Revisions of *The Unclassed*," *Nineteenth-Century Fiction* 8 (1953): 42–52; C. J. Francis, "*The Unclassed*," *The Gissing Newsletter* 10 (1974): 1–11; Jacob Korg, "Cancelled Passages in Gissing's *The Unclassed*," *Bulletin of the New York Public Library* 80 (1977): 553–58; and Robert S. Powell, "Gissing and 'the Impertinent Ego': A Comparison of Editions of *The Unclassed*," *The Gissing Newsletter* 16 (1980): 18–36.
6. George Gissing, *The Unclassed* (1895; rprt. London: Benn, 1930), pp. 46, 156. Subsequent page references to quotations from this edition appear parenthetically in the text and are preceded by the ab-

breviation U. At another point Gissing writes: "Dante saw nothing more fearful in any circle of hell" (U, p. 223), an allusion similarly evident in Schopenhauer's *The World as Will and Idea*, trans. R. B. Haldane and J. Kemp (London: Kegan Paul, Trench, Trübner, 1891), 1:419. This translation was a best-seller in turn-of-the-century England.

7. Critics have generally assumed that Waymark speaks for Gissing: see especially John Halperin, "How to Read Gissing," *English Literature in Transition* 20 (1977): 188–98; and Halperin, "On *The Unclassed* as Autobiography," *The Gissing Newsletter* 15 (1979): 3–11. This manner of interpretation is appropriate provided we keep in mind that Gissing was "trying out" a position through Waymark, that Waymark's views represent ideas Gissing was ambivalently entertaining rather than fully endorsing. This ambivalence permitted him on two occasions (23 and 25 June 1884) to refute his brother's equation of Waymark and his author: *Letters of George Gissing to Members of His Family*, ed. Algernon and Allen Gissing (Boston: Houghton Mifflin, 1927), pp. 140, 142.

8. Gisela Argyle, *German Elements in the Fiction of George Eliot, Gissing, and Meredith* (Frankfort, Germany: Lang, 1979), pp. 87–146.

9. C. J. Francis, "Gissing and Schopenhauer," *Nineteenth-Century Fiction* 15 (1960): 53–63.

10. George Gissing, "The Hope of Pessimism," in *George Gissing: Essays and Fiction*, ed. Pierre Coustillas (Baltimore: The Johns Hopkins University Press, 1970), p. 76. Subsequent page references to quotations from this essay appear parenthetically in the text and are preceded by the abbreviation HP.

11. Gissing may also be joking here, obliquely protesting his discomfort with the length of the three-volume novel. The first printed version of *The Unclassed* appeared in three volumes.

12. Anonymous, "Novels of the Week," *Athenaeum* no. 2957 (28 June 1884): 820–21. A more recent critic agrees that a failure in structure lies at "the core of Gissing's problems" as a novelist: Mabel Collins Donnelly, *George Gissing: Grave Comedian* (Cambridge: Harvard University Press, 1954), p. 74.

13. For my comments on pathos I am indebted to the excellent discussions by two of my colleagues: Warwick Wadlington, "Pathos and

Dreiser," *Southern Review* 7 (1971): 411–29; and Anthony Channell Hilfer, *The Ethics of Intensity in American Fiction* (Austin: University of Texas Press, 1981).

14. Schopenhauer, *The World as Will and Idea*, 3:267.

15. Whereas John Goode recognizes that the opening scene of the novel produces major narrative consequences, he objects to the ending and to "the mists of a dissolving conventional structure": *George Gissing: Ideology and Fiction* (London: Vision, 1970), pp. 72–79.

16. Jacob Korg makes this suggestion in *George Gissing: A Critical Biography* (Seattle: University of Washington Press, 1963), p. 67.

17. See M. H. Abrams, *Natural Supernaturalism: Tradition and Revolution in Romantic Literature* (New York: Norton, 1973), pp. 183–87; Timothy Materer, *Vortex: Pound, Eliot, and Lewis* (Ithaca: Cornell University Press, 1979); and William J. Scheick, "Schopenhauer, Maori Symbolism, and Wells's *Brynhild*," *Studies in the Literary Imagination* 13 (1980): 17–29.

18. *Arnold Bennett and H. G. Wells: A Record of a Personal and a Literary Friendship*, ed. Harris Wilson (Urbana: University of Illinois Press, 1960), p. 85.

19. Arnold Bennett, *Anna of the Five Towns* (Harmondsworth, England: Penguin, 1963), pp. 59, 235. Subsequent page references to quotations from this edition appear parenthetically in the text and are preceded by the abbreviation A.

20. *Letters of Arnold Bennett*, 2:172–75.

21. See J. E. Dearlove, "Artistic Control and an All-Embracing Compassion in *The Old Wives' Tale*," *Arnold Bennett Newsletter* 2, no. 2 (1977): 76–89. See also Roby E. Kinley, "Arnold Bennett's Social Conscience," *Modern Fiction Studies* 17 (1971): 513–24.

22. *The Journal of Arnold Bennett: 1896–1928* (New York: Viking, 1933), p. 300.

23. That Bennett was as much a Romantic as a realist has been remarked by critics, particularly by James G. Hepburn, who also sees *Anna* as the start of Bennett's eventually extensive use of religious symbolism: *The Art of Arnold Bennett* (Bloomington: Indiana University Press, 1963). See also Walter F. Wright, *Arnold Bennett: Romantic Realist* (Lincoln: University of Nebraska Press, 1971).

24. *The Journal of Arnold Bennett*, p. 22. See also Geoffrey West, *The*

Problem of Arnold Bennett (London: Joines and Steele, 1932), pp. 74–75.

25. On Bennett's therapeutic para-cultural angst, see William Bellamy, *The Novels of Wells, Bennett and Galsworthy: 1908–1910* (London: Routledge and Kegan Paul, 1971), pp. 144–64.

26. Bennett, "George Gissing," p. 724.

27. *Letters of Arnold Bennett: Volume I, Letters to J. B. Pinker*, ed. James Hepburn (London: Oxford University Press, 1966), p. 288.

28. In *Arnold Bennett: Primitivism and Taste* (Seattle: University of Washington Press, 1959), James Hall has remarked a different structure: "Once these two families have been introduced for what they are, the structure of the novel consists in their parallel claims upon Anna's interest leading to the parallel defiance by which she establishes her independence" (pp. 37–38).

29. Gustav Freytag, *Technique of the Drama*, trans. Elias J. MacEwan (Chicago: Scott, Foresman, 1894), pp. 114–40.

30. Letter of 23 April 1901 to George Sturt, *Letters of Arnold Bennett*, 2:151.

31. Documentation of Bennett's fascination with the theater appears in William J. Scheick, "Marketable Footle: Bennett and Wells's 'The Crime,'" *Cahiers Victoriennes et Edouardiennes* nos. 9/10 (October 1979): pp. 165–80.

32. Arnold Bennett, *The Author's Craft* (New York: Doran, 1914), p. 87.

33. *Arnold Bennett and H. G. Wells*, p. 86.

34. For example, Edward Garnett and H. G. Wells: *Letters of Arnold Bennett*, 2:166, 170. See also L. G. Johnson, *Arnold Bennett of the Five Towns* (London: Daniel, 1924), p. 68.

35. *The Journal of Arnold Bennett*, p. 101.

36. Wright, *Arnold Bennett: Romantic Realist*, p. 59.

37. This is a Schopenhauerian concept: see C. J. Francis, "Gissing's Characterization: Heredity and Environment," *Literary Half-Yearly* 3 (1962): 28–37. Although Adrian Poole errs in reporting that the revised printed version of *The Unclassed* exhibits "almost total excision of the Schopenhauerian element," he rightly remarks a breakdown in Gissing's management of Ida: *Gissing in Context* (London: Macmillan, 1975), pp. 64–69.

3. De-Forming In-Struction

1. An earlier version of this chapter appeared as "The De-Forming In-Struction of Wells's *The Wonderful Visit* and *The Sea Lady*," *English Literature in Transition* 30 (1987): 397–409.
2. *The Wonderful Visit*, in *The Works of H. G. Wells* (New York: Scribner's, 1924), 1:156, 248. Subsequent page references to quotations from this edition appear parenthetically in the text and are preceded by the abbreviation WV. Nordau's influence on Wells is discussed by Bernard Bergonzi, *The Early H. G. Wells: A Study of the Scientific Romances* (Manchester, England: Manchester University Press, 1961), pp. 4–7.
3. Early reviewers felt the force of this pessimism, as exemplified by W. L. Courtney, "Books of the Day," *Daily Telegraph* (London), 27 September 1895, p. 8, remarking the theme of the ruinous results of mixing the ideal and the practical. More recently, the ending of the romance has been interpreted as an expression of Wells's negative view of humanity's inability to achieve faith and love on earth: Antonina Vallentin, *H. G. Wells: Prophet of Our Day* (New York: Day, 1950), pp. 112–13. The weight of the conclusion of the novel is also remarked by Norman Nicholson, *H. G. Wells* (London: Barker, 1950). That a dark social Darwinism informs the book is noted by Norman and Jeanne Mackenzie, *H. G. Wells: A Biography* (New York: Simon and Schuster, 1973), p. 124.
4. This potentiality, albeit not the distinction between plot-structure and narrative-structure, was remarked in an early anonymous review in *Literary World* (Boston) 27 (1896): 251.
5. John R. Reed's claim that the narrator's intrusions in this work and others represent Wells's satirization of the novelist's practice and his need to be in the action of his works is too simplistic: *The Natural History of H. G. Wells* (Athens: University of Ohio Press, 1982), pp. 202–3.
6. For Bergonzi, the angel is like the Eloi in *The Time Machine* (1895) in representing the insufficiency of aestheticism (pp. 91–92), a view repeated by Frank McConnell, who sees the angel as a representative of "useless beauty" in a world ignorant of beauty (*The Science Fiction of H. G. Wells* [New York: Oxford University Press, 1981], pp. 40–42). To assert, however, that Wells satirizes

the angel's value is to miss the thrust of the narrative-structure of *The Wonderful Visit* in relation to its plot-structure.

7. *The Sea Lady* first appeared in July through December 1901 in *Pearson's Magazine*; it was printed as a book in 1902. In *Experiment in Autobiography* [New York: Macmillan, 1934], p. 393], Wells notes that he planned the novel in 1900, but does not suggest that he wrote it this early. The question of the date of composition arises mainly as a result of a comment, in a snide anonymous review of the book, that *The Sea Lady* was an old, rejected manuscript which now was published because of Wells's increased popularity: "Novels," *Saturday Review* (London) 94 (30 August 1902): 271–72.

8. The sources of Wells's use of these two figures have interested critics. The influences behind *The Wonderful Visit* have been said to include Swift [Alfred Borrello, *H. G. Wells: Author in Agony* [Carbondale: Southern Illinois University Press, 1972], p. 62], Ivan Karamazov's "The Grand Inquisitor" (Vallentin, *H. G. Wells: Prophet of Our Day*, p. 112], and Grant Allen's *The British Barbarians* (David Y. Hughes, "H. G. Wells and the Charge of Plagiarism," *Nineteenth-Century Fiction* 21 [1966]: 85–90), a book Wells reviewed (see *H. G. Wells's Literary Criticism*, ed. Patrick Parrinder and Robert M. Philmus [Sussex, England: Harvester, 1980], pp. 59–62). The influences behind *The Sea Lady* have been said to include Ibsen's "The Lady from the Sea" (John R. Reed, "The Literary Piracy of H. G. Wells," *Journal of Modern Literature* 7 [1974]: 537–42) and, in Wells's own admission in *Experiment in Autobiography* (p. 393), Mrs. Humphry Ward's *Marcella* (1894), although in both cases the endings of the earlier works have been reversed. Interestingly, both *The Wonderful Visit* and *The Sea Lady* have been identified as influences on Ford Madox Ford's *Mr. Apollo*: Arthur Mizener, *The Saddest Story: A Biography of Ford Madox Ford* (New York: World, 1971), pp. 154–55.

9. Although John Reed asserts that both *The Wonderful Visit* and *The Sea Lady* are "trivial productions" (*Natural History*, p. 6), usually and oddly the later book has not been taken as seriously as the earlier one. For Vallentin, *The Sea Lady* is evasive concerning human problems (p. 163) and for Ingvald Raknem, it is "a slight work" (*H. G. Wells and His Critics* [Torndheim, Norway: Boktry-

kueri, 1962], p. 51). The Mackenzies refer to it as "a poor piece of work" (p. 178), but they admit that it had a serious point to make. Just how serious both that point and the book were to Wells is indicated in *Experiment in Autobiography* (p. 401).

10. *The Sea Lady*, in *The Works of H. G. Wells* (New York: Scribner's, 1925), 5:426, 336, 367. Subsequent page references for quotations from this edition appear parenthetically in the text and are preceded by the abbreviation SL.

11. John Reed suggests that the mermaid represents Wells's attention to the aesthetic position (*Natural History*, p. 279, note 61), a point that should make us recall that the angel in the earlier romance represents the place of art.

12. *The Sea Lady* is hardly the "jeu d'esprit" Bergonzi says it is (*The Early H. G. Wells*, p. 21), and Wells's view of the seriousness of the work indicates that it is not (see note 9 above). Moreover, Wells elsewhere spoke of a frustrated love affair as an influence on this novel: *H. G. Wells in Love: Postscript to Experiment in Autobiography*, ed. G. P. Wells (London: Faber and Faber, 1984), p. 62. The dark nature of this romance is registered still more forcefully by Geoffrey West, who thinks *The Sea Lady* incorporates Wells's thoughts about suicide: *H. G. Wells* (London: Howe, 1930), p. 267.

13. William J. Scheick, "Schopenhauer, Maori Symbolism, and Wells's *Brynhild*," *Studies in the Literary Imagination* 13 (1980): 17–29.

14. *George Gissing and H. G. Wells: Their Friendship and Correspondence*, ed. Royal A. Gettmann (Urbana: University of Illinois Press, 1961), pp. 193, 208.

15. Even some early reviewers were discontented with the conclusion of *The Sea Lady*, but they did not suspect that this disappointment might have been a deliberate Wellsian effect. One anonymous critic thought that Wells was probably as surprised at his ending as is the reader ("Fiction," *Academy* 63 [9 August 1902]: 155–56). Closer to the mark, another anonymous reviewer sensed a gap between the initial satire in the novel and the concluding tragedy ("Novels," *Spectator* [London] 89 [16 August 1902]: 229–30).

16. On the influence of Schopenhauer on Melville, see Daniel Stempel and Bruce M. Stillians, "*Bartleby the Scrivener*: A Parable of Pessimism," *Nineteenth-Century Fiction* 27 (1972): 268–82.

17. Wells's struggle against his natural tendency toward pessimism is

discussed in Anthony West's "Men and Ideas: H. G. Wells," *Encounter* 8 (February 1957): 52–59; another, quite different version of this essay, with the same thesis, appeared as "The Dark World of H. G. Wells," *Harper's Magazine* 214 (May 1957): 18–73.

4. Compassion, Fictional Structure, and the Reader

1. Preliminary attempts to compare the two writers have appeared: e.g., Edward Wagenknecht, " 'Pessimism' in Hardy and Conrad," *College English* 3 (1942): 546–54. Contrasts have also emerged: e.g., Kellog W. Hunt, "*Lord Jim* and *The Return of the Native*: A Contrast," *English Journal* 49 (1960): 447–56. An earlier version of this chapter appeared as "Schopenhauerian Compassion, Fictional Structure, and the Reader: The Example of Hardy and Conrad," *Twilight of Dawn: Studies in English Literature in Transition*, ed. O M Brack, Jr. (Tucson: University of Arizona Press, 1987), pp. 45–67, 212–18; by permission from the University of Arizona Press, copyright 1987.

2. The problem is manifest in G. W. Sherman, *The Pessimism of Thomas Hardy* (Rutherford, New Jersey: Fairleigh Dickinson University Press, 1976), and is redressed in Ian Gregor, "*Jude the Obscure*," in *Imagined Worlds: Essays in Some English Novels and Novelists in Honor of John Butt*, ed. Maynard Mack and Ian Gregor (London: Methuen, 1968), pp. 237–56; and in J. Hillis Miller, *Thomas Hardy: Distance and Desire* (Cambridge: Harvard University Press, 1970), p. 44.

3. See, e.g., Harvey Curtis Webster, *On a Darkling Plain: The Art and Thought of Thomas Hardy* (Chicago: University of Chicago Press, 1947); J. O. Bailey, "Hardy's Visions of the Self," *Studies in Philology* 56 (1959): 74–101; and Bailey, "Evolutionary Meliorism in the Poetry of Thomas Hardy," *Studies in Philology* 60 (1963): 569–87.

4. William R. Rutland, *Thomas Hardy: A Study of His Writings and Their Background* (Oxford: Blackwell, 1938).

5. Eden Phillpotts, "Thomas Hardy and Schopenhauer," in *From the Angle of 88* (London: Hutchinson, 1951), pp. 68–76; Evelyn Hardy, *Thomas Hardy: A Critical Biography* (London: Hogarth Press, 1954), pp. 53, 286.

6. For example, Paul Neugebauer, *Schopenhauer in England: Mit*

Besonderer Berücksichtigung Seines Einfluesses auf die Englische Literatur (Berlin: Doktordruck-Graphisches Institute Paul Funk, 1932), pp. 33–39.

7. As argued by Friedrich Wild, *Die Englische Literatur der Gegenwart seit 1870: Drama und Roman* (Wiesbaden: Drosburen, 1931), pp. 118–21, 159–68.

8. As remarked by Samuel C. Chew, "Homage to Thomas Hardy," *New Republic* 23 (21 June 1920): 22–26; Webster, *On a Darkling Plain*, pp. 196–98; and Bailey, "Evolutionary Meliorism," p. 574.

9. Carl J. Weber, "Hardy's Copy of Schopenhauer," *Colby Library Journal* 4 (1957): 217–24.

10. Edward Wright, "The Novels of Thomas Hardy," *Quarterly Review* 199 (1904): 499–523; Harold Williams, "Thomas Hardy (1840)," in *Two Centuries of the English Novel* (London: Smith and Elder, 1911), pp. 283–303. See also Helen Garwood, *Thomas Hardy: An Illustration of the Philosophy of Schopenhauer* (Philadelphia: Winston, 1911).

11. Barry Schwartz, "*Jude the Obscure* in the Age of Anxiety," *Studies in English Literature* 10 (1970): 793–804.

12. Thomas Hardy, *Jude the Obscure*, ed. C. H. Sisson (Harmondsworth, England: Penguin, 1978), p. 451. Page references to quotations from this edition appear parenthetically in the text and are preceded by the abbreviation JO.

13. Arthur Schopenhauer, *The World as Will and Idea*, trans. R. B. Haldane and J. Kemp (London: Kegan Paul, Trench, Trübner, 1891), 2:411.

14. Lawrence Jones, "Thomas Hardy's 'Idiosyncratic Mode of Regard,'" *English Literary History* 42 (1975): 437.

15. Compare Schopenhauer, *The World as Will and Idea*, 1:142, 419.

16. Schopenhauer, *The World as Will and Idea*, 1:400.

17. Schopenhauer, *The World as Will and Idea*, 3:430–31.

18. How the Will turns against itself is, by Schopenhauer's own admission, a difficult and paradoxical concept. On *Maya*, however, Schopenhauer explains: "Maya is . . . this visible world in which we are, a summoned enchantment, an inconstant appearance without true being, like an optical illusion or a dream, a veil which surrounds human consciousness, something of which it is equally

false and true to say that it is and that it is not" (*The World as Will and Idea*, 2:9).

19. As contended by Roy Morrell, *Thomas Hardy: The Will and the Way* (Singapore: University of Malaya Press, 1965).

20. Arnold Bennett, "Tendencies of Modern Literature," *T. P.'s Weekly* 14 (1909): 7–10.

21. As remarked by Jerome Hamilton Buckley, *The Triumph of Time* (Cambridge: Harvard University Press, 1966), p. 63.

22. Herbert Leslie Stewart, "Thomas Hardy as a Teacher of His Age," *North American Review* 208 (1918): 584–96.

23. In a thought-provoking, if sometimes mistaken, essay by Morton Dauwen Zabel, "Hardy in Defense of His Art: The Aesthetic of Incongruity," *Southern Review* 6 (1940): 125–49.

24. Phillpotts, "Thomas Hardy and Schopenhauer," pp. 74–75.

25. Schopenhauer, *The World as Will and Idea*, 1:485–90, 530–31.

26. Schopenhauer, *The World as Will and Idea*, 1:455, 490.

27. Lewis P. Horne, "The Art of Renunciation in Hardy's Novels," *Studies in the Novel* 4 (1972): 556–67. See also Norman Holland, "*Jude the Obscure:* Hardy's Symbolic Indictment of Christianity," *Nineteenth-Century Fiction* 9 (1954): 50–60.

28. Schopenhauer (*The World as Will and Idea*, 1:526–28) endorses the idea of Christian renunciation, which he believes to have been improved upon by Buddhism and, finally, by his own philosophy.

29. Richard Benvenuto unconvincingly argues that Jude's love implies the intrinsic value, overlooked by the narrator, of individual lives: "Modes of Perception: The Will to Live in *Jude the Obscure*," *Studies in the Novel* 2 (1970): 31–41.

30. Phillpotts, "Thomas Hardy and Schopenhauer," p. 69.

31. On the whole critics have disapproved of Hardy's characterization of Father Time. A cautionary note is in order, for possibly the idea of children appearing more aged than those of preceding generations may have had greater currency at the end of the nineteenth century than we now suspect. Theodore Roosevelt's sister Anna was thought by her family not only to be competent beyond her years but also to look tired, painfully sad, and years older than she was: David McCullough, *Mornings on Horseback* (New York: Simon and Schuster, 1981), pp. 32–35.

32. Geoffrey Thurley, *The Psychology of Hardy's Novels: The Nervous and the Statuesque* (St. Lucia: University of Queensland Press, 1975), pp. 184–85.

33. Ian Gregor, "Hardy's World," *English Literary History* 38 (1971): 274–93.

34. Miller, *Thomas Hardy: Distance and Desire*, p. 208; cf. pp. 259–60.

35. The conflicting points of view are typified by "Architecture and Thomas Hardy," *Architect and Building News* (London) 119 (20 January 1928): 119–21, 139, 147; and William Lyon Phelps, "The Novels of Thomas Hardy," *North American Review* 190 (1909): 502–14.

36. Edmund William Gosse, "Mr. Hardy's New Novel," *Cosmopolis* 1 (1896): 60–69.

37. Florence Emily Hardy, *The Later Years of Thomas Hardy, 1892–1928* (New York: Macmillan, 1930), p. 40.

38. See Fernand Lagarde, "À propos de la construction de *Jude the Obscure*," *Caliban* 3 (1966): 185–214.

39. See David Lodge, "*Jude the Obscure*: Pessimism and Fictional Form," in *Critical Approaches to the Fiction of Thomas Hardy*, ed. Dale Kramer (London: Macmillan, 1979), pp. 193–201. A parallelism of repeated scenes in the novel that serves as cropped and bordered framing passages (in a photographic sense) is discussed in Mary Ann Caws's *Reading Frames in Modern Fiction* (Princeton: Princeton University Press, 1985), pp. 73–85.

40. See Margaret Makar, "Hardy's Poetry of Renunciation," *English Literary History* 45 (1978): 303–24; and Daniel R. Schwarz, "Beginnings and Endings in Hardy's Major Fiction," in *Critical Approaches*, pp. 17–35.

41. "The typological vision generally accompanies a profound determinism that always threatens to become pessimism": Sherman, *The Pessimism of Thomas Hardy*, p. 230. Cf. Schopenhauer, *The World as Will and Idea*, 3:227.

42. On the allusions to Christ, see Lodge, "*Jude the Obscure*: Pessimism and Fictional Form," pp. 193–201.

43. Schopenhauer, *The World as Will and Idea*, 3:267.

44. Miller, *Thomas Hardy: Distance and Desire*, p. 39.

45. Daniel R. Schwarz, "The Narrator as Character in Hardy's Major

Fiction," *Modern Fiction Studies* 18 (1972): 155–72; and Dale Kramer, "*Jude the Obscure:* Doctrine or Distanced Narrative," in *Thomas Hardy: The Forms of Tragedy* (Detroit: Wayne State University Press, 1975), pp. 136–65. The opposite view, that the narrator insists on his knowledge and on the reader's dependence upon him, is argued by John Sutherland, "A Note on the Teasing Narrator of *Jude the Obscure*," *English Literature in Transition* 17 (1974): 159–62. Sutherland is right to note the narrator's manner of getting the reader's attention, but the reason for this behavior lies in Hardy's apparent intention to disrupt the reader's usual acceptance of the viewpoint of a third-person narrative voice.

46. See Miller, *Thomas Hardy: Distance and Desire*, p. 6.
47. Robert W. Stallman, "Hardy's Hour Glass Novel," *Sewanee Review* 55 (1947): 283–96; reprinted in *The House James Built and Other Literary Studies* (East Lansing: Michigan State University Press, 1961), pp. 53–63.
48. Where it is remarked as the true symbol of nature: Schopenhauer, *The World as Will and Idea*, 3:267.
49. Frank R. Giordano, Jr., "*Jude the Obscure* and the *Bildungsroman*," *Studies in the Novel* 4 (1972): 580–91.
50. For example, J. Pitt, "Things and Other Things: Letters to Living Authors—VII. Mr. Thomas Hardy," *Good Words* 43 (1902): 647–76; Wilfred S. Durant, "The Disciple of Destiny," *Fortnightly Review* 91 (1909): 1117–24.
51. Usually for inadequate catharsis: e.g., W. M. Payne, "Recent Fiction," *Dial* 20 (1 February 1896): 76–77; Williams, "Thomas Hardy (1840)," pp. 283–303.
52. D. H. Lawrence, "Hardy's 'Prédilection d'artiste,'" in *Phoenix* (New York: Viking, 1936), pp. 434–40. See also Arthur Mizener, "*Jude the Obscure* as Tragedy," *Southern Review* 6 (1940): 193–213. The opposite position is taken by Zabel, "Hardy in Defense of His Art," pp. 125–49, and Ted R. Spivey, "Thomas Hardy's Tragic Hero," *Nineteenth-Century Fiction* 9 (1954): 179–91.
53. Pathos is the dominant mode of literary naturalism, a problematical term but one that has often been applied to Hardy: e.g., D. F. Hannigan, "Mr. Thomas Hardy's Latest Novel," *Westminster Review* 142 (1896): 136–39; William Newton, "Chance as Employed by Hardy and the Naturalists," *Philological Quarterly* 30 (1951):

154–75; and Newton, "Hardy and the Naturalists: Their Use of Physiology," *Modern Philology* 49 (1951): 28–41.

54. A sense of tragedy would indeed be evoked if, as David DeLaura has argued, Jude fails because of the gap between his humanitarian ideal and his historical situation: "The Ache of Modernism in Hardy's Later Novels," *English Literary History* 34 (1967): 380–99 (cf. Miller, *Thomas Hardy: Distance and Desire*, p. 213); it would be evoked as well if, as Bert G. Hornback has argued, Hardy's characters are not determined, but have the power to choose: *The Metaphor of Chance: Vision and Technique in the Works of Thomas Hardy* (Athens: Ohio University Press, 1971).

55. James R. Kincaid, "Hardy's Absences," in *Critical Approaches*, p. 205. Hardy's use of a pseudo-tragic figure who cheats the reader of fulfillment of expectations generated by the novel is discussed in Robert Evans's "The Other Eustacia," *Novel* 1 (1968): 251–59. And on the frustration of the reader's search for an authoritative interpretation of the text, see Ramón Saldívar's "*Jude the Obscure:* Reading and the Spirit of the Law," *English Literary History* 50 (1983): 607–25.

56. Miller formulates Hardy's artistic objective: "The wider, the more detached, the more impersonal, the more disinterested, the more clear and objective a man's view is the closer he will come to seeing the truth of things as they are"; art "holds things at a distance and imitates in another pattern the objective patterns in the outside world which have held his attention through their power to generate an emotional fascination. Such an art is at once a reaction to the external world, and a protection against it. It is a transformation of the reaction into a shape which imitates it at a distance." Two clarifications are useful here: one, the external world of phenomena evinces patterns only insofar as conscious minds seek those patterns and in the process posit them, a situation which is also true of art; second, artistic detachment for Hardy, at least in *Jude*, also seems to require profound philosophical compassion.

57. Thomas Hardy, *Tess of the D'Urbervilles: A Pure Woman Faithfully Presented* (1891), ed. William E. Buckler (Boston: Houghton-Mifflin, 1960), p. xxii. Pertinent is James Gindon's discussion of Hardy in *Harvest of the Quiet Eye: The Novel of Compassion* (Bloomington: Indiana University Press, 1971), pp. 78–101.

58. Schopenhauer, *The World as Will and Idea*, 1:271.

59. John A. Palmer, *Joseph Conrad's Fiction: A Study in Literary Growth* (Ithaca: Cornell University Press, 1968).

60. Edward Said, *Joseph Conrad and the Fiction of Autobiography* (Cambridge: Harvard University Press, 1966). See also Ian Watt, "*Heart of Darkness* and Nineteenth-Century Thought," *Partisan Review* 45 (1978): 108–19.

61. John Galsworthy, *Castles in Spain* (New York: Scribner's, 1927), p. 121; Galsworthy, "Reminiscences of Conrad: 1924," in *Two Essays on Conrad* (Cincinnati: Ebbert and Richardson, 1930), p. 52. See also Bruce Johnson, *Conrad's Models of Mind* (Minneapolis: University of Minnesota Press, 1971), pp. 41–53. Johnson argues that Conrad repudiated Schopenhauer's denial of the ego through selflessness and emphasized art celebrating individual will as the crucial source of value. In "Conrad's 'Pessimism' Re-Examined" (*Conradiana* 2, no. 3 [1969–70]: 25–38) Lee M. Whitehead suggests that critics have overestimated the presence of Schopenhauerian pessimism in Conrad's writings.

62. William W. Bonney, *Thorns and Arabesques: Contexts for Conrad's Fiction* (Baltimore: The Johns Hopkins University Press, 1980), pp. 3–11.

63. See Lillian Feder, "Marlow's Descent Into Hell," *Nineteenth-Century Fiction* 9 (1955): 280–92; and Robert O. Evans, "Conrad's Underworld," *Modern Fiction Studies* 2 (1956): 56–62.

64. Jospeh Conrad, *Heart of Darkness*, ed. Robert Kimbrough (New York: Norton, 1971), pp. 14, 17. Page references to quotations from this edition appear parenthetically in the text and are preceded by the abbreviation HD.

65. On the role of the harlequinesque Russian in the novel, see C. F. Burgess, "Conrad's Pesky Russian," *Nineteenth-Century Fiction* 18 (1963): 189–93; John Edward Hardy, " 'Heart of Darkness': The Russian in Motley," in *Man in the Modern Novel* (Seattle: University of Washington Press, 1964), pp. 17–33; Mario D'Avanzo, "Conrad's Motley as an Organizing Metaphor in *Heart of Darkness*," *College Language Association* 9 (1966): 289–91; John W. Canario, "The Harlequin in *Heart of Darkness*," *Studies in Short Fiction* 4 (1967): 225–33; Jack Helder, "Fool Convention and Conrad's Hollow Harlequin," *Studies in Short Fiction* 12 (1975): 361–

68; and Emily K. Yoder, "The Demon Harlequin in Conrad's Hell,"
Conradiana 12 (1980): 88–92.

66. The *danse macabre* figures in Cecil Scrimgeour's "Jimmy Wait and
the Dance of Death: Conrad's *Nigger of the Narcissus*," *Critical
Quarterly* 7 (1965): 339–52.

67. Alan Warren Friedman errs, I think, in believing that "Marlow
seizes grotesquely on the morality of ideas" but is correct in adding that for Marlow ideas "remain . . . problematical, a matter
demanding continual struggle, always in motion": "Conrad's Pica-
resque Narrator: Marlow's Journey from *Youth* to *Chance*," in
Multivalence: The Moral Quality of Form in the Modern Novel
(Baton Rouge: Louisiana State University Press, 1978), pp. 108–
40. Others have singled out certain ideas which Marlow is said to
endorse, even imperialism (Leo Gurko, *Joseph Conrad: Giant in
Exile* [London: Macmillan, 1962], pp. 148–53; and Jonathan Rose,
The Edwardian Temperament, 1895–1919 [Athens: Ohio University Press, 1986], p. 153). On other features of Conrad's attitude
toward ideas, see Allan O. McIntyre, "Conrad on the Function of
the Mind," *Modern Language Quarterly* 25 (1964): 187–97.

68. William Bysshe Stein, "The Lotus Posture and *Heart of Dark-
ness*," *Modern Fiction Studies* 2 (1956–57): 167–70. See also Stein,
"Buddhism and 'Heart of Darkness,' " *Western Humanities Review* 11 (1957): 281–85; Stein, "Bodhisattva Scenario," *Orient/
West* 9 (1964): 37–46; and H. C. Brashers, "Conrad, Marlow, and
Gautama Buddha: On Structure and Theme in *Heart of Darkness*,"
Conradiana 1, no. 3 (1969): 63–72. In "*Heart of Darkness* and the
Problem of Emptiness" (*Studies in Short Fiction* 9 [1972]: 387–
400) Bruce Johnson explains, "The emptiness, indeed nothingness,
so often intimated, continually eludes the Buddha defense, which
after all is equipped for nearly the opposite kind of threat." This
position supersedes the issue of whether Marlow in some sense
discovers a moral universe: e.g., Jerome Thale, "Marlow's Quest,"
University of Toronto Quarterly 24 (1955): 351–58; and Robert F.
Haugh, *Joseph Conrad: Discovery in Design* (Norman: University
of Oklahoma Press, 1957), pp. 35–40.

69. Arnold Bennett, "The Progress of the Novel," *Realist* 1 (1 April
1929): 3–11. A distinction between simple and complex altruism
in *Heart*, albeit with inadequate grounding in the Schopenhauerian

context with which the discussion begins, is provided by Lawrence Graver, *Conrad's Short Fiction* (Berkeley: University of California Press, 1969). See also Garry Geddes, "The Structure of Sympathy: Conrad and the Chance That Wasn't," *English Literature in Transition* 12 (1969): 175–88; and Juliet McLauchlan, "The 'Something Human' in *Heart of Darkness*," *Conradiana* 9 (1977): 115–25.

70. See Bruce R. Stark, "Kurtz's Intended: *The Heart of Darkness*," *Texas Studies in Literature and Language* 16 (1974): 535–55; and James Ellis, "Kurtz's Voice: The Intended as 'The Horror,'" *English Literature in Transition* 19 (1976): 105–10.

71. See Gerald B. Kauvar, "Marlow as Liar," *Studies in Short Fiction* 5 (1968): 290–92. Other features of the lie are discussed by Kenneth A. Bruffee, "The Lesser Nightmare: Marlow's Lie in *Heart of Darkness*," *Modern Language Quarterly* 25 (1964): 322–29; and Ted E. Boyle, "Marlow's 'Lie' in 'Heart of Darkness,'" *Studies in Short Fiction* 1 (1964): 159–63.

72. See Robert Kimbrough's annotations: *Heart of Darkness*, pp. 33, 57. That, finally, *Heart* is more concerned with adjustment than with judgment is noted by Sanford Pinsker, *The Language of Joseph Conrad* (Amsterdam: Rodopi, 1978), p. 48. See also John A. McClure, "The Rhetoric of Restraint in *Heart of Darkness*," *Nineteenth-Century Fiction* 32 (1977): 310–26.

73. See Stark, "Kurtz's Intended," pp. 546–48.

74. This dual position is what Peter J. Glassman slights when he concludes that Marlow and the narrator, recoiling from experience, define themselves by an aversion to life: "The Horror: *Heart of Darkness*," in *Language and Being: Joseph Conrad and the Language of Personality* (New York: Columbia University Press, 1976), pp. 198–249. On the other hand, involvement does not necessarily imply Conrad's disapproval of Marlow's response, which is the doubtful position of Eliose Knapp Hay, *The Political Novels of Joseph Conrad: A Critical Study* (Chicago: University of Chicago Press, 1963); nor does it necessarily imply Conrad's endorsement of the importance of values, which is remarked by Suresh Raval, *The Art of Failure: Conrad's Fiction* (Boston: Allen and Unwin, 1986), p. 42.

75. On Kurtz and Marlow as artists, see Elsa Nettels, "'Heart of Darkness' and the Creative Process," *Conradiana* 5, no. 2 (1973): 66–73.

76. On the correspondence between this passage and Conrad's method, see Stewart C. Wilcox, "Conrad's 'Complicated Presentations' of Symbolic Imagery in *Heart of Darkness*," *Philological Quarterly* 39 (1960): 1–17. On Marlow's trouble with language, see Bruce Johnson, "Names, Naming, and the 'Inscrutable' in Conrad's *Heart of Darkness*," *Texas Studies in Literature and Language* 12 (1971): 675–88; and on Marlow's use of language as both an abstraction and as a tool of vision, see Jerry Wasserman, "Narrative Presence: The Illusion of Language in *Heart of Darkness*," *Studies in the Novel* 6 (1974): 327–38; and Jeremy Hawthorn, *Joseph Conrad: Language and Fictional Self-Consciousness* (Lincoln: University of Nebraska Press, 1979), pp. 7–36.

77. Roger Ramsey, "The Available and the Unavailable 'I' in Conrad and James," *English Literature in Transition* 14 (1971): 137–45; Elsa Nettels, "James and Conrad on the Art of Fiction," *Texas Studies in Literature and Language* 14 (1972): 524–43; and Ian Watt, "Marlow, Henry James, and 'Heart of Darkness,'" *Nineteenth-Century Fiction* 33 (1978): 159–74. On the void at the center see Albert Spaulding Cook, "Plot as Discovery: Conrad, Dostoevski, and Faulkner," in *The Meaning of Fiction* (Detroit: Wayne State University Press, 1960), pp. 202–41. On the unsatisfied reader, permanently off-balance, see Adena Rosmarin, "Darkening the Reader: Reader-Response Criticism and *Heart of Darkness*," *Joseph Conrad: Heart of Darkness*, ed. Ross C. Murfin (New York: St. Martin's Press, 1989), pp. 148–71.

78. The topography of the telling, oscillating between a collective "we" and an isolated "I," is discussed in L. J. Morrissey's "The Tellers in *Heart of Darkness*: Conrad's Chinese Boxes," *Conradiana* 13 (1981): 141–48. On Conrad's notion of art as a means of bringing things together and of keeping them at a distance, see J. Hillis Miller, "Joseph Conrad," in *Poets of Reality: Six Twentieth-Century Writers* (Cambridge: Harvard University Press, 1965), pp. 13–67.

79. On Melville and Conrad, see Frank MacShane, "Conrad on Melville," *American Literature* 29 (1958): 463–64; Jesse D. Green, "Diabolism, Pessimism, and Democracy: Notes on Melville and Conrad," *Modern Fiction Studies* 8 (1962): 287–305; and Leon F.

Seltzer, "Like Repels Like: The Case of Conrad's Antipathy for Melville," *Conradiana* 1, no. 3 (1969): 101–5.

5. Structure and Ethics in Contemporary Fiction

1. On Wilde's influence, too, on Borges, see Richard Ellmann, *Oscar Wilde* (New York: Knopf, 1988).
2. In *Loss of Self in Modern Literature and Art* ([New York: Vintage Books, 1962], p. 14) Wylie Sypher correlates the diminishment of humanism with the loss of authorial belief in individual character. According to Alain Robbe-Grillet, "The novel of characters belongs entirely to the past": *For a New Novel: Essays on Fiction*, trans. Richard Howard (New York: Grove Press, 1965), p. 28.
3. Vladimir Nabokov, *The Defense* (New York: Capricorn, 1970), pp. 8–9. Page references for subsequent quotations from this edition appear parenthetically in the text and are preceded by the abbreviation D. On the importance of structure in the work of Robbe-Grillet, see George H. Szanto, *Narrative Consciousness: Structure and Perception in the Fiction of Kafka, Beckett, and Robbe-Grillet* (Austin: University of Texas Press, 1972), pp. 149–56. On the ethical implications of Nabokov's work, see Ellen Pifer, *Nabokov and the Novel* (Cambridge: Harvard University Press, 1980).
4. Vladimir Nabokov, *Despair* (New York: Capricorn, 1970), pp. 131–32, 195. Page references for subsequent quotations from this edition appear parenthetically in the text and are preceded by the abbreviation Dr.
5. Vladimir Nabokov, *Invitation to a Beheading* (New York: Crest, 1960), pp. 75–76, 89.
6. Robert Scholes, *Fabulation and Metafiction* (Urbana: University of Illinois Press, 1979), pp. 213–18. See also Georg Lukacs, *Writer and Critic and Other Essays*, trans. Arthur D. Kahn (New York: Grosset and Dunlap, 1971), p. 69.
7. Robert N. Wilson, *The Writer as Social Seer* (Chapel Hill: University of North Carolina Press, 1979), pp. 13–16; Wayne C. Booth, *The Company We Keep: An Ethics of Fiction* (Berkeley: University of California Press, 1988).
8. Arnold L. Weinstein, *Vision and Response in Modern Fiction* (Ithaca: Cornell University Press, 1974), p. 273. It is less certain,

however, that Weinstein is correct in remarking that for these novelists the human ability to respond to this void by inventing meaning is intrinsically good (p. 276).

9. Ernest Sandeen, *"The Wings of the Dove* and *The Portrait of a Lady:* A Study of Henry James's Later Phase," *PMLA* 69 (1954): 1060–75. See also, on the conflict of the aesthetic and the moral in James, Dorothea Krook, *The Ordeal of Consciousness in Henry James* (Cambridge: Cambridge University Press, 1962), and J. T. Laird, "Cracks in Precious Objects: Aestheticism and Humanity in *The Portrait of a Lady," American Literature* 52 (1981): 643–48.

10. Paul B. Armstrong, "How Maisie Knows: The Phenomenology of James's Moral Vision," *Texas Studies in Literature and Language* 20 (1978): 517–37.

11. E. M. Forster, *Aspects of the Novel* (1927; rprt. New York: Harcourt, Brace and World, 1954), pp. 153–65.

12. Ian Watt, "Marlow, Henry James, and 'The Heart of Darkness,'" *Nineteenth-Century Fiction* 33 (1978): 159–74.

13. James was much influenced by Hawthorne, about whose work he wrote a study.

14. Joseph Conrad, *Lord Jim* (Harmondsworth, England: Penguin, 1949), p. 264; cf. p. 254. Page references for subsequent quotations from this edition appear parenthetically in the text and are preceded by the abbreviation LJ.

15. Edward W. Said, *Joseph Conrad and the Fiction of Autobiography* (Cambridge: Harvard University Press, 1966), p. 156; Jeremy Hawthorn, *Joseph Conrad: Language and Fictional Self-Consciousness* (Lincoln: University of Nebraska Press, 1979), p. 48.

16. Pertinently Paul de Man observes, all "literary 'form' is the result of the dialectical interplay between the prefigurative structure of the foreknowledge and the intent at totality of the interpretative process"; thus, "form is never anything but a process on the way to its completion" through the temporal factor provided by the inquiring and constitutive mind of the reader. *Blindness and Insight: Essays in the Rhetoric of Contemporary Criticism* (London: Oxford University Press, 1971), p. 31.

Index